MY HEART'S DESIRE

~

LIVING EVERY MOMENT
in the WONDER *of* WORSHIP

DAVID
JEREMIAH

ABOUT
DR. DAVID JEREMIAH
AND TURNING POINT

D r. David Jeremiah is the founder of Turning Point, a ministry committed to providing Christians with sound Bible teaching relevant to today's changing times through radio and television broadcasts, audio series, books, and live events. Dr. Jeremiah's common-sense teaching on topics such as family, prayer, worship, angels, and biblical prophecy forms the foundation of Turning Point.

David and his wife, Donna, reside in El Cajon, California, where he serves as the senior pastor of Shadow Mountain Community Church. David and Donna have four children and twelve grandchildren.

In 1982, Dr. Jeremiah brought the same solid teaching to San Diego television that he shares weekly with his congregation. Shortly thereafter, Turning Point expanded its ministry to radio. Dr. Jeremiah's inspiring messages can now be heard worldwide on radio, television, and the Internet.

Because Dr. Jeremiah desires to know his listening audience, he travels nationwide holding ministry rallies and events that touch the hearts and lives of many people. According to Dr. Jeremiah, "At some point in time, everyone reaches a turning point; and for every person, that moment is unique, an experience to hold onto forever. There's so much changing in today's world that sometimes it's difficult to choose the right path. Turning Point offers people an understanding of God's Word as well as the opportunity to make a difference in their lives."

Dr. Jeremiah has authored numerous books, including *Escape the Coming Night* (Revelation), *The Handwriting on the Wall* (Daniel), *Overcoming Loneliness, Grand Parenting, The Joy of Encouragement, Prayer—The Great Adventure, God in You* (Holy Spirit), *When Your World Falls Apart, Slaying the Giants in Your Life, My Heart's Desire, Sanctuary, Forward, Everything You Need, Where Do We Go From Here, Captured by Grace, Grace Givers, Signs of Life,* and *God Loves You: He Always Has—He Always Will.*

ABOUT THIS STUDY GUIDE

The purpose of this Turning Point study guide is to reinforce Dr. David Jeremiah's dynamic, in-depth teaching and to aid the reader in applying biblical truth to his or her daily life. This study guide is designed to be used in conjunction with Dr. Jeremiah's *My Heart's Desire* audio series, but it may also be used by itself for personal or group study.

STRUCTURE OF THE LESSONS

Each lesson is based on one of the messages in the *My Heart's Desire* compact disc series and focuses on specific passages in the Bible. Each lesson is composed of the following elements:

- *Outline*

The outline at the beginning of the lesson gives a clear, concise picture of the topic being studied and provides a helpful framework for readers as they listen to Dr. Jeremiah's teaching.

- *Overview*

The overview summarizes Dr. Jeremiah's teaching on the passage being studied in the lesson. Readers should refer to the Scripture passages in their own Bibles as they study the overview. Unless otherwise indicated, Scripture verses quoted are taken from the New King James Version.

- *Application*

This section contains a variety of questions designed to help readers dig deeper into the lesson and the Scriptures, and to apply the lesson to their daily lives. For Bible study groups or Sunday school classes, these questions will provide a springboard for group discussion and interaction.

- *Did You Know?*

This section presents a fascinating fact, historical note, or insight that adds a point of interest to the preceding lesson.

USING THIS GUIDE FOR GROUP STUDY

The lessons in this study guide are suitable for Sunday school classes, small-group studies, elective Bible studies, or home Bible study groups. Each person in the group should have his or her own study guide.

When possible, the study guide should be used with the corresponding compact disc series. You may wish to assign the study guide lesson as homework prior to the meeting of the group and then use the meeting time to listen to the CD and discuss the lesson.

FOR CONTINUING STUDY

For a complete listing of Dr. Jeremiah's materials for personal and group study call 1-800-947-1993, go online to www.DavidJeremiah.org, or write to: Turning Point, P.O. Box 3838, San Diego, CA 92163.

Dr. Jeremiah's *Turning Point* program is currently heard or viewed around the world on radio, television, and the Internet in English. *Momento Decisivo*, the Spanish translation of Dr. Jeremiah's messages, can be heard on radio in every Spanish speaking country in the world. The television broadcast is also broadcast by satellite throughout the Middle East with Arabic subtitles.

Contact Turning Point for radio and television program times and stations in your area. Or visit our website at www.DavidJeremiah.org.

My Heart's Desire

When James Earl ("Jimmy") Carter, Jr., was the 39th president of the United States, he delivered the eulogy at the funeral service for former Vice President Hubert Humphrey. In a reverse characterization of Humphrey, he read a list of the seven chief sins which he found on a trip to India, written on the wall of a memorial to Gandhi: Wealth without works, pleasure without conscience, knowledge without character, commerce without morality, science without humanity, worship without sacrifice, and politics without principle. Humphrey, Carter said, was not perfect, but he was a man whose life was free, in the long view, from the stain of these sins.

Did you note the next to the last in the list—worship without sacrifice? Is it really a sin to worship without sacrifice? That question demands that we know what worship is. And when we discover the biblical perspective on worship of God, we reach perhaps an even stronger conclusion: Worship without sacrifice is really not worship at all. And yet, all over the world millions of Christians gather each Lord's day to "worship" God. Are those services true worship services? What does it mean to worship "sacrificially"?

Perhaps part of the problem in recognizing the nature of true worship is that we have relegated it to the Sunday morning hour. In fact, according to Scripture, all of life is to be lived as an act of worship. When we recognize that fact, we see how it is impossible to worship without sacrifice. The apostle Paul exhorts us to "present [our] bodies a living sacrifice, holy, acceptable to God, which is [our] reasonable service [of worship]" (Romans 12:1).

Paul's language, of course, is rooted in the Old Testament where sacrifice was part and parcel of worship. No Israelite would think of coming to worship without an offering to God in hand. An animal might be brought as a sin, guilt, burnt, or fellowship offering. Or part of the harvest might be brought as a grain offering, accompanied by a drink offering or freewill offering. The showbread, oil for the lampstand, and incense for the altar were also brought as offerings.

One would not think of going to worship God without giving up something of his own as a sacrifice to God.

The reason is rooted in the definition of worship itself: Worth-ship, in the simplest of terms. God is worthy of our honor, praise, and thanksgiving because of who He is and what He has done. To return to Paul's words, the sacrifice we bring to Him today is our entire life, a living sacrifice to Him. We say, "Lord, because of who You are and what You have done for me, I give myself wholly to you. To do anything less would suggest that I place less than infinite value on who You are."

As A. W. Tozer said, worship is "the missing jewel" of the church. God's people need to recapture the meaning of worship and develop a vision for all of life as a sacrificial act of worship. It is to that end that this study guide has been prepared for you. We will discuss the priority of worship as well as look at its meaning in-depth— especially why worship demands sacrifice. Practically, we will look at acts of worship through music and song. We will fast-forward to the future and look at worship of the Father and the Lamb in eternity. And we will see why worship is our certain shield against spiritual attack and times of despair.

When you are gone, will you be remembered as a person whose life was lived as a sacrifice to God? Gaining a biblical perspective on worship is the first step toward that goal.

THE IMPORTANCE OF WORSHIP

Selected Scriptures

*In this lesson we discover the centrality
of worship in the spiritual life.*

OUTLINE

The hurry-up world we live in means people rarely take time to read
the directions. And the same is unfortunately true in the Christian
life. We forge ahead to service, fellowship, study, evangelism, and
missions without ever stopping to complete step #1: Worship.

  I.   Worship Is the Priority Commandment of God

 II.   Worship Was the Pattern of the Old Testament

III.   Worship Was the Practice of the New Testament

 IV.   Worship Is Our Primary Responsibility Before God

  V.   Worship Is the Place Where God Is at Home

 VI.   Worship Is the Prerequisite to Effective Service

VII.   Worship Is the Panacea for Discouragement

VIII. Worship Is the Passion of God

IN PREPARATION FOR THIS LESSON, BE SURE TO READ CHAPTER THREE
IN THE BOOK, *My Heart's Desire.*

I t has been said that too many Christians worship their work, work at their play, and play at their worship. What we do on Sundays we call worship . . . but is it really? For many people the subject of worship is an enigma. They come to services and sing, but they sense something is missing. They pray and talk with God each day, but find themselves wondering if perhaps there is something they failed to learn about their life with God.

Why is worship important? Because it is the highest priority in God's Word.

WORSHIP IS THE PRIORITY COMMANDMENT OF GOD

Exodus 20 records the giving of the Ten Commandments, with the very first instruction saying: "I am the Lord your God. . . . You shall have no other gods before Me. You shall not make for yourself a carved image—any likeness of anything that is in heaven above, or that is in the earth beneath, or that is in the water under the earth; you shall not bow down to them nor serve them. For I, the Lord your God, am a jealous God" (Exodus 20:2–5). Before He gave any other commandment, God established that the greatest concern was understanding the importance of worship.

When Jesus was asked to state the greatest commandment, He quoted Deuteronomy 6:4–5: "Hear, O Israel: The Lord our God, the Lord is one! You shall love the Lord your God with all your heart, with all your soul, and with all your strength." Worship is at the top of God's priority list.

WORSHIP WAS THE PATTERN OF THE OLD TESTAMENT

When you begin to read the Scriptures and study the people of the Old Testament, you cannot read far before you begin to understand that worship was the pattern of their lives. The Lord Himself designed the first worship center. He was very specific; it took seven chapters to describe how He wanted it built. He made it portable, and designed it to be a visual aid for the worshiping Israelite. The tabernacle was the center of the encampment of God's people. Next to it were the priests who led worship; further away were the Levites who were involved in service, and outside of them were the people. It was a way of showing that God was to be at the center of His people in worship as a way of life.

WORSHIP WAS THE PRACTICE OF THE NEW TESTAMENT

You can find a priority on worship throughout the New Testament. Take a look at the Gospel according to Matthew. At the outset we are met with the coming of the Messiah. The response of the wise men, as recorded in Matthew 2:11, is that they came into the house and "saw the young Child with Mary His mother, and fell down and worshiped Him."

In Matthew 8:2 we are told of a leper who approaches Jesus: "And behold, a leper came and worshiped Him, saying, 'Lord, if You are willing, You can make me clean.'" In Matthew 9:18 we meet a certain ruler who came to Jesus and "worshiped Him." Matthew 15:25 tells of the woman of Canaan who "worshiped Him, saying, 'Lord, help me!'"

We find Jesus with His disciples in Matthew 14:33. He has just walked on water and calmed the seas, and the response of His followers is that "those who were in the boat came and worshiped Him, saying, 'Truly You are the Son of God.'"

In the Lord's final days on earth, He went up on a mountain with His disciples and "they worshiped Him" (Matthew 28:17). In just one book we have the consistent pattern that wherever Jesus was, He was known as the Son of God. Men and women worshiped the Lord; it was the pattern and practice of the New Testament.

The Book of Revelation reveals that in heaven the worship of God will be practiced continually: "'Blessing and honor and glory and power be to Him who sits on the throne, and to the Lamb, forever and ever!' Then the four living creatures said, 'Amen!'" (Revelation 5:13–14)

WORSHIP IS OUR PRIMARY RESPONSIBILITY BEFORE GOD

The most essential thing we can do is not soul-winning, service, tithing, or teaching. It is worship. King David said that, above all things, he desired to worship God. "One thing have I desired of the Lord, that will I seek: that I may dwell in the house of the Lord all the days of my life, to behold the beauty of the Lord, and to inquire in His temple" (Psalm 27:4). David, the soldier-poet, says that of all things, he desires most to worship God because in this one thing all other things are found.

For the apostle Paul there was only one theme: "That I may know Him and the power of His resurrection, and the fellowship of His sufferings, being conformed to His death" (Philippians 3:10). The worship of Christ was the central concern of his life.

Perhaps the clearest illustration occurs in the story of Mary and Martha. Mary was a quiet person. Martha was a busy, active person. Sisters, they lived together in the same house. "Now it happened as they went that He entered a certain village; and a certain woman named Martha welcomed Him into her house. And she had a sister called Mary, who also sat at Jesus' feet and heard His word. But Martha was distracted with much serving, and she approached Him and said, 'Lord, do You not care that my sister has left me to serve alone? Therefore tell her to help me.' And Jesus answered and said to her 'Martha, Martha, you are worried and troubled about many things. But one thing is needed, and Mary has chosen that good part, which will not be taken away from her'" (Luke 10:38–42).

Jesus says, in effect, that Martha was running around like a chicken with its head cut off trying to do things, as though the busy person is the one serving God most effectively. But Mary is just sitting there at His feet, worshiping and adoring God; doing the only thing really necessary.

Worship needs to be in the center of all that we do. It cannot be peripheral. It cannot be an addendum. It has to be the center of all that we do. Yes, we need to witness and we need to work, but until worship is central, all those other things will be a struggle and will not flow as they ought from our worship of the Lord.

WORSHIP IS THE PLACE WHERE GOD IS AT HOME

Psalm 22:3 tells us that God inhabits the praises of His people. He lives in the midst of our praise. When the Lord is worshiped, then we see Him in His natural environment; He is at home.

Of course God exists everywhere, but He is not always manifest everywhere. His manifest presence comes to us when He is praised. C. S. Lewis once wrote that "it is in the process of being worshiped that God communicates His presence to men . . . even in Judaism the essence of the sacrifice was not really that men gave bulls and goats to God, but that by their so doing God gave Himself to men."

Perhaps you have experienced the wonderful presence of God during a special time of worship. As you were singing, praying, praising, and worshiping the Lord, you felt His presence closer to you than ever before—that is what the psalmist is describing!

Worship causes the presence of God to be felt and experienced by His people. If you really want to sense the presence of God in your church meetings, praise Him as best you can.

WORSHIP IS THE PREREQUISITE TO EFFECTIVE SERVICE

What is more important, to worship God or to serve Him? By virtue of what we do in our churches, you would think that the really important thing was to serve God. The modern church seems preoccupied with service, using it as a sort of barometer of spirituality. But Satan tempted Jesus by asking for His worship, not His service: "All these things I will give You if You will fall down and worship me" (Matthew 4:9). Satan understands the correct order—the one you worship is the one you will serve. And keep in mind Christ's response in verse 10: "You shall worship the Lord your God, and Him only you shall serve." Worship is the prerequisite to effective service. Oswald Chambers once wrote, "If you have not been worshiping . . . when you get into work you will not only be useless but a tremendous hindrance."

Amy Carmichael, founder of Dohnavur Mission in South India, insisted that when the large chapel was built on their compound, it have two spires. The spire at the front was to represent worship. The spire at the rear was to represent service. Whenever those spires are seen, all are reminded that worship precedes service. Perhaps this shows some relationship to the fact that Amy Carmichael was able to labor for forty years without a furlough.

WORSHIP IS THE PANACEA FOR DISCOURAGEMENT

Worship is something God uses in the lives of His people to help them in their own discouragement. You cannot be occupied with both despair and the worthiness of God. When your heart is caught up in the worship of God, it does something to you inwardly, dispelling the spirit of heaviness. The prophet Isaiah said, "The Spirit of the Lord God is upon me . . . He has sent me to heal the brokenhearted, to proclaim liberty to the captives . . . to comfort all who mourn, to console those who mourn in Zion, to give them beauty for ashes, the oil of joy for mourning, the garment of praise for the spirit of heaviness" (Isaiah 61:1–3).

Discouragement is one of Satan's greatest weapons today. So the Scripture warns us not to grow faint or lose heart, but to worship God. Paul and Silas were once arrested, flogged, thrown into prison, and locked in stocks. It must have been a discouraging, defeating time. How did they respond? They started to pray and sing hymns to God! As a result of their worship, there was an earthquake and the doors of the prison were blown open.

WORSHIP IS THE PASSION OF GOD

There are times in life when you don't know for sure what God wants you to do . . . but you can always be certain that when you worship God, you are in His will. Jesus told the woman at the well, "The hour is coming, and now is, when the true worshipers will worship the Father in spirit and truth; for the Father is seeking such to worship Him" (John 4:23). God in heaven is looking throughout the earth for people to worship Him.

And the best news of all is that as we worship God, He will fill up our lives. Then we will begin to understand the words of Jesus to that woman: "If you knew the gift of God, and who it is who says to you, 'Give Me a drink,' you would have asked Him, and He would have given you living water. . . .Whoever drinks of the water that I shall give him will never thirst. But the water that I shall give him will become in him a fountain of water springing up into everlasting life" (John 4:10, 14).

When Lawrence of Arabia was in Paris with some of his Arab friends after World War I, he took them to see the sights of the city. His friends showed little interest in the Louvre, the Arch of Triumph, or Napoleon's tomb. The thing that really interested them was the faucet in their bathtub. They spent much time turning it on and off; they thought it was wonderful. All they had to do was turn the handle and they could get all the water they wanted.

When they were leaving Paris, Lawrence found them in the bathroom with wrenches, trying to get the faucet off so they could take it with them. "You see," they said, "it is very dry in Arabia. What we need are faucets. If we have them, we will have all the water we want." Lawrence had to explain to them that the effectiveness of the faucet depended on the water system to which it was attached.

Our study of worship reminds us that the effectiveness of all that we do in the church is not to be found in outward activity or service, but in the One who stands behind it. The One whom we serve. The One deserving of our worship.

Note

1. John Ayto, *Dictionary of Word Origins*, p. 577.

APPLICATION

1. Read Exodus 20:1–17.

   a. What is the point of the first commandment? (verse 3)

   b. What is the focus of the second commandment? (verse 4)

   c. Taken together, toward whom are the first four commandments directed? (verses 2–11)

   d. To whom are the last six commandments directed? (verses 12–17)

   e. What does this grouping of the commandments suggest to you about the order of the believer's priorities in life?

   f. What is our human tendency regarding these priorities?

2. How is worship, as an act of bowing down or humbling oneself, illustrated in the following verses:

   a. Genesis 18:2

   b. 1 Samuel 24:8

   c. Ruth 2:10

   d. Genesis 37:5, 9–10

   e. Exodus 34:8

   f. Isaiah 2:20

   g. Isaiah 44:15, 17

3. What do you learn about worship in the early church from the following verses?

   a. John 20:19; Acts 20:7

   b. 1 Corinthians 16:2

c. Colossians 4:16

d. 1 Corinthians 14:14–16

e. Ephesians 5:19

f. Colossians 3:16

g. 1 Corinthians 11:18–34

h. 1 Corinthians 14:40

4. How are personal and corporate worship different?

   a. What is the most meaningful aspect of corporate worship? Personal worship?

   b. What do you think would enhance the corporate worship experience at your church?

   c. What contribution do you make to the corporate worship experience at your church?

DID YOU KNOW?

The English word "worship" originated as a nonreligious compound noun meaning "worthiness." It was the result of combining two existing English terms, the adjective "worth" and the noun suffix "—ship," which meant state or condition. The resulting compound noun, "worthship," first meant distinction, credit, or dignity, which gradually became respect or reverence. It is easy to see how "worthship" could move from secular to religious usage (although "Your Worship" is still a British formalism used to address dignitaries, akin to American, "Your Honor" when addressing a judge.) The verb form, "to worship," originated in the 12th century and appears in religious contexts in the 13th.[1]

WHAT IS WORSHIP?

Selected Scriptures

*In this lesson we learn
what true worship is, and is not.*

OUTLINE

It is politically correct to say that everyone is free to worship God in his own way. Granted, people are free to "ascribe worth" to anyone or anything. But Scripture is clear: There is only one God, and He alone is to be worshiped, in spirit and in truth.

I. **What Worship Is Not**
   A. Ignorant Worship
   B. Improper Worship
   C. Idolatrous Worship
   D. Inferior Worship

II. **What Worship Is**
   A. Worship Is a Response of Obedience to God
   B. Worship Is a Reverent Submission to God
   C. Worship Is the Result of the Death of Christ
   D. Worship Is a Reflection of Your Whole Life

IN PREPARATION FOR THIS LESSON, BE SURE TO READ CHAPTER FIVE
IN THE BOOK, *My Heart's Desire.*

We owe much of our interest in worship to A. W. Tozer, who was the first, in modern times, to publish a book on this topic. He referred to worship as "the missing jewel" of the church, a phrase copied by many. Little known by his contemporaries, his books began to be published after his death and people recognized his grasp of the church. In his book *Worship*, he said:

> Man was made to worship God. God gave man a harp and said, "Here, above all creatures that I have made and created I have given you the largest harp. I put more strings on your instrument and I have given you a wider range than I have given to any other creature. You can worship me in a manner that no other creature can." And when he sinned man took that instrument and threw it down in the mud and there it has lain for centuries, rusted, broken, unstrung; and man, instead of playing a harp like the angels and seeking to worship God in all of his activities, is ego-centered and turns in on himself and sulks and swears and laughs and sings, but it's all without joy and without worship. . . .Worship is the missing jewel in modern evangelicalism. We're organized; we work; we have our agendas. We have almost everything, but there's one thing that the churches, even the Gospel churches, do not have: that is the ability to worship. We are not cultivating the art of worship. It's the one shining gem that is lost to the modern church, and I believe we ought to search for this until we find it.[1]

As a pastor, I have come to realize that worship is the ultimate priority for which all of us were created. How then shall we go about it? What does it mean to worship? What kinds of worship does God accept and what kinds does He reject? What ways of expressing our worship to God are legitimate?

WHAT WORSHIP IS NOT

There are certain kinds of worship that God does not accept.

Ignorant Worship

First, it is important to recognize that God does not accept ignorant worship. When Jesus was talking to the Samaritan woman in John 4 about worship He said, "You worship what you do not know. . ." How can you truly worship something without knowing what it is? Paul struck a similar theme when he was preaching to the Athenians in Acts 17. "You people are very religious," he said. "As I walked around and observed your objects of worship I even found an altar with this inscription: To The Unknown God." How do you worship a god you don't know? Paul calls that ignorant worship.

All across the country last Sunday, churches were filled with people who walked in to worship something they did not know. People engaged in ignorant worship, and nothing really happened in their church or in their lives. They went through the external motions without ever really understanding the internal workings, and nothing happened because God does not accept ignorant worship. Worship is knowing God and worshiping Him; and if we do not know God, we cannot worship Him.

Improper Worship

Second, God does not accept improper worship. There are many biblical illustrations of improper worship, but perhaps the key passage is Romans 1. Paul, writing to the church in Rome, talks about the culture and its devolution of man. He explains that man has taken the creative work of God, which was given as a testimony to the greatness and might of God, and instead of worshiping the Creator to whom creation points, has instead worshiped the creation itself. Because of that, Paul says "God gave them up."

What a terrible thing to consider—God giving up on someone. God said that because they did not see beyond the creation to the Creator, to whom worship was due, and instead lifted up created things and worshiped them, He gave them up. Their rejection of God and embracement of the world was improper, so He let them go to their own devices until ultimately they were destroyed.

Idolatrous Worship

Third, God does not accept idolatrous worship. Do you know what an idol is? It is something you worship instead of God. It is anything you allow to get between you and your worship of the true God. There are many who have icons and statues that represent God, and they use them to worship. That is idolatry, for God says we are not ever to bring anything between our worship of God and ourselves. We are to worship Him and Him only.

Exodus 32 tells us that when Moses went up the mountain to get the Law, the people became idolatrous. They took all their gold jewelry, melted it down, and made a golden calf. They wanted something they could see, feel, and touch to help them worship God.

It was idolatry, and God did not accept it. Thousands died because they violated the concept of worship.

It is easy to let things come between God and ourselves. Some people worship crucifixes. Others wear things around their necks or place objects on the dashboards of their car. I believe some evangelicals worship the Bible, rather than use it as the means for knowing how to worship God. He wants to be worshiped from pure hearts, and anything we put between God and us is an idol.

Inferior Worship

Fourth, God does not accept inferior worship. Malachi was a very strong, impassioned prophet of God who wrote to the post-exilic Jews about how they had allowed their worship of the Lord to dissolve into empty ritual. This preacher stood up in front of these Jews and said, in effect, "You bring to God animals that you would never be allowed to present to your governor as payment for your taxes. You don't bring God the best. You bring Him the leftovers—the lame. You go out to your flock and find some mangy old goat and bring it to God and call it worship!" Malachi warned the people that God is a great God and we are to give Him the best we have. God wants the firstfruits of our lives, not the leftovers. He wants the best we can present to Him in terms of our gifts, our money, and our abilities. If you don't have a commitment to excellence, you don't understand worship. Worship is taking the best we have and bringing it to God as our offering to Him.

Disastrous things have happened to people who didn't worship correctly. Nadab and Abihu offered "strange fire" to the Lord and were killed in a moment. King Saul grew impatient, offered God an improper sacrifice, and lost his kingdom. The people of Israel created a golden calf and saw thousands die as punishment. It is imperative that we find out how God wants to be worshiped and offer Him our best.

WHAT WORSHIP IS

Worship Is a Response of Obedience to God

God has not given us the option to worship Him or not to worship Him. Worship is a command that God has given to us. It is a responsibility that all of us have. Consider the words of the Psalmist:

"Give unto the Lord the glory due to His name; worship the Lord in the beauty of holiness" (Psalm 29:2).

"Let us come before His presence with thanksgiving; let us shout joyfully to Him with psalms. . . . Oh come, let us worship and bow down; let us kneel before the Lord our Maker" (Psalm 95:2, 6).

"For the Lord is great and greatly to be praised . . . Honor and majesty are before Him; strength and beauty are in His sanctuary. . . . Oh, worship the Lord in the beauty of holiness!" (Psalm 96:4, 6, 9)

According to the Word of God, He is to be loved by His creatures with all their hearts, souls, and minds. He is to be praised, blessed, gloried in, feared, and exalted. He is to be extolled, thanked, and rejoiced in. There are hundreds of reminders in Scripture that we don't have an option. If we are going to be obedient children, we will worship God. Your first priority in attending church is not to see what you can get out of the sermon but what you can give back to God through your exercise of worship in obedience to His Word. Not to do that is to miss everything God has for you.

Worship Is a Reverent Submission to God

The root word in Hebrew that we translate "worship" really means "to bow down." The practice of bowing is an outward sign of reverence. Worship is a recognition and celebration of who God is. Bowing down and honoring Him is a way to give Him glory. When we bow down before God, we acknowledge that He is greater than we are; and by this acknowledgement we give glory back to Him.

Perhaps the purest illustration of worship in Scripture is depicted in Revelation 4:10–11: "The twenty-four elders fall down before Him who sits on the throne and worship Him who lives forever and ever, and cast their crowns before the throne, saying: 'You are worthy, O Lord, to receive glory and honor and power; for You created all things, and by Your will they exist and were created.'"

That is worship—giving back to God that which He deserves. In Roman times, when a king was conquered he was brought to Rome to prostrate himself before the emperor. He was required to fall down and cast his crown before Caesar's feet. This was his act of total submission, of abnegating himself to the emperor. The apostle John is saying that what they did to Caesar, we do to God. We come to God, bow down before Him, submit to Him, and declare His greatness. That is worship. It is done in reverent submission to the Lord.

Worship Is the Result of the Death of Christ

Today we can worship in a new way because we are redeemed by the shed blood of Jesus Christ. Do you remember Jesus talking with the woman of Samaria? She wanted to argue about where you should worship. "Lord, I understand the Samaritans think we should worship in Samaria, but the Jews think we should worship in Jerusalem." But Jesus replied, "The hour is coming when true worshipers will worship me neither here nor there, but they will worship in spirit and truth." When Christ died on the cross, and the veil separating the Holy of Holies was torn in two, the worship of God was radically changed. No longer does a man have to go to a priest. No longer does he have to be in a special place. Because Christ died to pay the penalty for all of our sin, now we can come in the priesthood of every believer and worship God because of His sacrifice.

That is why corporate worship is a celebration. Christ forgave us all of our sins and gave us His righteousness, a home in heaven, the Holy Spirit to live in our hearts, the Word of God to guide us each day, Christian friends to encourage us, and a church to celebrate these truths with others. That's why we can't always be somber and just sing slow, sad songs! We must fill our worship with joy, with celebrating. We are celebrating our redemption in Jesus Christ. Worship is the response of a heart that is excited about the God who is served.

Worship Is a Reflection of Your Whole Life

What happens in your worship is a microcosm of all that you are and do. Paul put it this way: "Present your bodies a living sacrifice, holy, acceptable to God, which is your reasonable service" (Romans 12:1). God says that when we come to Him and give Him our lives, we are saying, "Lord, here is this instrument of worship and praise, and I want it to be played all week long for Your honor and glory, so that everything I do, everything I say, everywhere I go, everything I think is an outgrowth of my love for You and an expression of my worship for You, my great God."

When we come together on Sunday and sing, we are saying, "Lord, we praise You and give You our lives." We listen to God and obey Him. We reach out to one another in love. The quality of our worship here is a reflection of our relationship with God. Our worship, like our lives, has one central focus: honoring and glorifying God.

Note

1. A. W. Tozer, Worship, *Christian Publications*, n.d., pp. 12, 23–24.

APPLICATION

1. Note what is ignorant, improper, idolatrous, or inferior about the worship mentioned in the following passages:

   a. Matthew 4:9

   b. Matthew 5:19

   c. John 4:22

   d. Acts 7:42–43

   e. Acts 17:23

   f. Acts 19:27

   g. Colossians 2:18

   h. Revelation 9:20

   i. Revelation 13:8, 12, 15

   j. Revelation 19:10; 22:8

2. Read Romans 1:18–32.

   a. What is happening to those who have failed to worship God? (verse 18)

b. Why are those who do not worship God without excuse? (verses 19–20)

c. Everyone gives glory (worships) something or someone. How does Paul characterize the ascribing of worship to the wrong thing(s)? (verses 21–23)

d. Instead of worshiping the Creator, what do idolaters worship? (verse 25)

e. What is God's ultimate response toward those who misdirect their worship? (verses 24, 26, 28)

f. What are three things that characterize those who actively worship idols? (verses 24, 26, 28)

g. Why are the characteristics mentioned in verses 29–31 out of character for the true worshiper of God?

3. Why would some people be "driven" to worship the creation instead of the Creator? (Deuteronomy 4:19)

    a. What role can spiritual deception play in false worship? (Deuteronomy 11:16)

    b. Why is it wrong to worship the right person (God) in the wrong way? (Deuteronomy 12:2–4)

    c. Why did God specify the place and manner in which He was to be worshiped? (Deuteronomy 12:5–7)

    d. What is wrong with the often-heard idea that people should worship God "each in their own way"? (Deuteronomy 12:8)

    e. How did Jesus correct the thinking of a woman who had good intentions regarding worship, but bad information? (John 4:21–25)

f. Why is it not narrow-minded in our modern cultures to say that all worship which did not originate with the Jews is misguided and false? (John 4:22)

g. Why would the "last fruits" of the harvest (or from our lives) be inappropriate to bring to the worship of God? (Deuteronomy 26:10)

4. In what way(s) should worship be connected with joy in the life of the Christian? (Philippians 3:3) How strong is that connection in your own life?

DID YOU KNOW?

As Paul walked around in the hyper-religious city of Athens, he encountered an altar with the inscription *Agnosto Theo*, "To the Unknown God." The second-century geographer Pausanias and the third-century philosopher Philostratus both mention altars to unknown gods in Athens (meaning in general or a specific altar, such as Paul mentions, we don't know). The reasoning of the Greeks in setting up such an altar was this: It was a safety precaution. Thinking that any god for whom an altar was not erected would extract vengeance upon the city, the Athenians erected an "anonymous" altar to placate any unknown god they had overlooked.

THE WONDER OF WORSHIP

Selected Scriptures

In this lesson we learn why wonder is the gateway to worship.

OUTLINE

When was the last time you stopped and reveled in a sunset? Or explored the intricacies of a flower in the garden? Many people have lost the ability to be amazed at the greatness of God. There is a direct correlation between childlike wonder at God and the ability to worship Him for who He is.

I. **The Anticipation of Wonder**

II. **An Anthology of Wonder**
  A. The Wonder of the Creation of the World
  B. The Wonder of the Culmination of the World
  C. The Wonder of the Creature Himself

III. **The Antithesis of Wonder**

IV. **The Attitudes of Wonder**
  A. We Must Be Passionate About Living Every Moment in the Wonder of Worship
  B. We Must Know God Rather Than Simply Know About Him
  C. We Must Serve God Rather Than Simply Identifying With Him
  D. We Must Worship God Daily, Which Will Require Adjustments and Sacrifices

V. **The Application of Wonder**

IN PREPARATION FOR THIS LESSON, BE SURE TO READ CHAPTERS TWO AND SIXTEEN IN THE BOOK, *My Heart's Desire.*

THE ANTICIPATION OF WONDER

A story from the annals of the Apollo space flight program is a fitting introduction to the topic of wonder and worship. A reporter named Jacob Needleman was one of many journalists who gathered in Florida for the launch of Apollo 17 in 1975. Prior to the evening launch, the reporters had gathered to socialize. Their conversation was consistent with the world of the press and media—some sarcasm, some cynicism, lots of jokes and laughter. It's hard to amaze veteran journalists with anything. They've seen it all.

When the giant Atlas rocket finally lifted off the launch pad, the reporters were blinded by a shield of orange light from the rocket engines. When the sound waves reached them, the reporters were jarred to the bone by the deafening roar. The earth, and their bodies standing on it, shook from the force. The sound continued, though it grew fainter, as the rocket rose into the night sky. Within a matter of moments it seemed the rocket had become just a pinprick of light, like a distant star. And then it was gone, disappearing into the night of space.

As Needleman looked around at his fellow reporters, no one uttered a sound. They stood with mouths open looking at the sky. No more wisecracks, no more jokes, no more "show me" attitude. These hardened journalists had seen something awe-inspiring. When they finally began to move about, their conversation was quiet, almost reverent. It seemed, if only for a moment, that they had been in the presence of something so much bigger and more powerful than themselves that they were shocked into wonder.[1]

If we think journalists in the 1970s were hardened cynics, what should we say about our own generation? The dark Florida sky into which Apollo 17 disappeared is a picture of the darkness of our times. We are a people characterized not by awe or wonder but by cynicism and empty nihilism. NASA's space shuttles traveled into space regularly and it hardly merited a mention on the evening news. We have seen so much progress, and so much evil, that we have become hardened to almost everything.

The 20th century began with anticipation of Utopia. Science, technology, and wealth were supposed to usher in an era of unbridled prosperity and peace. When war did break out, World War I was labeled "The War to End All Wars"—the civilized world's final conflict. But wars continued, and Utopia became a dream instead of a possibility. When twin, monolithic towers in New York City, symbols of economic prosperity in the world's most powerful city, were toppled by a handful of rogue terrorists, we were introduced into a new age. September 11, 2001, became the day which changed the world forever. We were chilled by horror and dread beyond anything we might have considered before. We wondered if we could ever live again without looking over our shoulders. Many have lost all hope in mankind, predicted decades ago by G. K. Chesterton: "The world is not lacking in wonders, but in a sense of wonder."

The place of wonder in worship is critical; and before we can worship, we must learn again to wonder. Worship is never the product solely of a rational mind. It is not a quantitative or technical experience which can be planned or analyzed by a computer—the way much of our current life can be. Worship and wonder bring us to the end of ourselves, the end of our abilities. We can only stand in wondrous awe before our Almighty God and let His power and presence change us.

I hope you will recapture a sense of wonder and awe in this study—not unlike that of a little child. Remember the times when you were awed as a child? The first sight of the ocean or a chain of mountains? A longed-for Christmas present—maybe a toy train that snaked all around the living room? The sight and sound of a huge stadium filled with screaming fans at your first big-league sporting event? If we find wonder in those kinds of events, all the more should we find wonder in God. Do you ever wonder? How long has it been since you've been like a child again, gaping with wide eyes? How would it change your life if you could live like that every day? How would it change the people around you?

So many lives are lived apart from wonder. Instead of wandering through the emptiness, we should be wondering at the fullness of God and His love. God created you to wonder at Him. Your heart's desire, even if you haven't come to realize it, is to live every moment in the wonder of worship.

An Anthology of Wonder

God's wondrous acts stand like bookends at the beginning and ending of history. Genesis and Revelation are gateways to worship inspired by wonder.

The Wonder of the Creation of the World

None of us was there to witness it, but Genesis tells us how God fashioned the world, and everything in it, at the beginning of time

We can read about how God said, "Let there be light"—and light came into being. He separated the waters above and below the firmament, placed the sun, moon, and stars in the sky, and filled the air with birds, the sea with fish, and the land with animals of all kinds. When we contemplate what He did "in the beginning," or contemplate His creation today, we should be moved to declare with God, "It is good!" Not only is it good, it is perfect—or at least it was when God created it. And creation still bears the mark of His perfection. Even our ability to marvel at His creation is marvelous— an evidence of the image of God in which we were created.

Wonder requires emotion—the involvement of our soul and imagination. If you and your favorite canine friend are looking at the same sunset, only one of you will be moved. In fact, only one of you will be looking at the sunset. While your dog is busy scratching at a flea, you will be fixed on the beauty and majesty of the sun sinking beneath the horizon. There is no simpler way to illustrate what sets man apart from the animals than that. You laugh, you cry, you stand in awe—but no animal does. There is nothing material— no sets of neurons which evolved by chance—that causes our soul to wonder at God's handiwork or brings tears to our eyes when we hear beautiful music.

Our ability to wonder is itself a gateway through which we can encounter God; it is an open door to worship, an occasion to take stock of true spiritual perspective. God has filled the heavens with billboards; and if we fail to see them, the fault lies in us, not Him. Albert Einstein put it this way: "The most beautiful thing we can experience is the mysterious. It is the source of all true art and science. He to whom the emotion is a stranger, who can no longer pause to wonder and stand rapt in awe, is as good as dead: his eyes are closed."[2]

The Wonder of the Culmination of the World

Creation and culmination are indeed the bookends of Scripture. We marvel at the world God created and we can marvel at how He will bring this heaven and earth to its close. God gave the Revelation to John the Apostle to write down so that anyone, anytime could marvel at His work in culminating this world.

The Wonder of the Creature Himself

Not only is the Bible a wonderful book, it is a book filled with wonder from beginning to end. At the very heart of the Bible is the Book of Psalms. Nowhere is wonder a more constant theme than in the psalms:

O Lord, our Lord,
How excellent is Your name in all the earth,
Who have set Your glory above the heavens! . . .
When I consider Your heavens, the work of Your fingers,
The moon and the stars, which You have ordained,
What is man that You are mindful of him,
And the son of man that You visit him?
For You have made him a little lower than the angels,
And You have crowned him with glory and honor.
Psalm 8:1, 3–5

This psalm is a favorite of many because it captures in such simple words how we feel when we look into the heavens. We find ourselves in company with David who gazed into the heavens so many nights as a young shepherd in the fields. No wonder he asked why God was inclined to pay attention to us humans in light of the glories of the rest of His creation. David realized that we are part of the glorious creation of God. We are small, but significant—tiny creatures whom He adores.

The Bible begins with the wonder of creation, implanted deeply within us. It ends with the wonderful culmination of God's final judgment. And in the very center, with the psalms, are songs of praise and wonder. His central written revelation to us is just as crammed with heaven as creation itself. But the challenge is this: We are flawed, fallen creatures, prone to pluck at forbidden fruit rather than bask in worship as God designed us. How do we confront these limitations?

THE ANTITHESIS OF WONDER

Sin has distorted our sense of wonder. All of our perceptions about God, our world, and even ourselves have been twisted by sin. The opposite of wonder is cynicism, and if we are not careful we will fall into its trap. We spend more time exposed to cynicism each day than to anything else. Movies, television, the media, the conversation around us—it is filled with the opposite of wonder.

Many people felt that after the terrorist attacks of September 11, 2001, things would change, that America would become a different, even better, place. And there was a change for a while. But when things returned to normal, sarcasm and cynicism resumed their pre-9/11 place in our culture. Our culture doesn't view anything with eyes of innocence anymore. We have been disappointed by politicians and preachers and so find it hard to believe that anyone is telling the truth, doing what they do with pure motives. Our culture doesn't know God, of course, and so they cynically lump Him in with everything else they distrust. If we are not careful, our childlike ability to marvel at God will go the way of the cynics.

It's not a new problem, of course. Jesus encountered cynics in His day at every turn. The Pharisees could not see the kingdom of God because of their blind cynicism about Jesus and His teachings and miracles. Even the disciples fell short in seeing the big picture—so He gave them a smaller one. He held up a little child as the model for approaching God. This was an affront to the Pharisees and the disciples; they thought children were not worthy of serious attention. But Jesus said that whoever does not receive the kingdom of God as a little child would never enter it (Luke 18:16–17).

What did He mean? When Jesus made that statement, the disciples had been arguing about who would be the greatest in Jesus' kingdom, so the implication is obvious. Humility . . . wonder . . . innocence. These things go hand in hand when contemplating God and His purposes. We do not need sophisticated, worldly faith. We need the perspective of a little child—faith which believes God for who He is and what He has done. Like a child on Christmas morning, we need to be in awe of God every moment of every day.

THE ATTITUDES OF WONDER

What do we need to know to approach God once again as little children?

We Must Be Passionate About Living Every Moment in the Wonder of Worship

To live in God's presence in this world is to swim against the stream of our culture. You must have an overpowering drive to know God intimately to overcome the pressure of this world. You must be willing to spend each day in intimate relationship with Him. The path begins with the passion.

We Must Know God Rather Than Simply Know About Him

This point is obvious but essential. You can be filled with information about God, and even about knowing Him, and still not know Him intimately. At some point you have to put down the books about God and approach the throne of God. The journey to wonder begins in the mind but does not end until it reaches the heart.

We Must Serve God Rather Than Simply Identifying With Him

Growth in faith comes through doing the things that Jesus would do. Serve someone today and tomorrow, and see if you don't encounter God in a more powerful way. Almost paradoxically, retreating into deep fellowship with God ultimately means having more experience with people. People are God's agenda. Service will help you reestablish the wonder in your worship.

We Must Worship God Daily, Which Will Require Adjustments and Sacrifices

Sacrifice is at the heart of worship. Living every moment in the wonder of worship will require alterations in your thinking, your priorities, and your approach to every portion of your life. Some of this will be painful. You'll be building a profile of obedience, and you'll be clearing away impediments that block the wonderful view. In the end, you'll count it all as loss for the perfect joy of knowing God.

The wonder of worship brings wonderful rewards. You'll experience joy and devotion toward God and a greater connectedness to family and friends. Cynicism will be replaced by a childlike approach to Christ and His kingdom.

THE APPLICATION OF WONDER

There will be days for you (there are for all of us), when your commitment and decision to worship God will be your strength more than a sense of joy. You may wonder some days whether God is really with you, days when you don't seem to sense His presence. But those who seek Him will find Him, so don't give up (Proverbs 8:17; Jeremiah 29:12–13). Stop and smell the spiritual roses and you will find God. Enjoying His handiwork in creation, encountering Him in the solitude of a sunset, meeting Him in the life of another person—these are all ways to nurture your sense of wonder.

Those who come to realize God's love overflow with love themselves. Realizing God's love allows you to love yourself in a biblical fashion. And those who are secure in themselves are the only ones who can give God's unconditional love to others.

Notes

1. From Bill Moyers, *A World of Ideas II*, PBS Video, quoted in Rusty Freeman, "Night of Wonder," Journal for Preachers, Advent 2000, 11.

2. Quoted in S.M. Ulam, *Adventures of a Mathematician* (New York: Charles Scribner's Sons, 1976), 289.

1. Read Psalm 8:1–9.

    a. How would you describe David's sense of wonder about God and His works? (verse 1)

    b. How has God confounded the cynical and the "wise" through children? (verse 2a)

    c. What irony is there in God using children to "silence the enemy and the avenger"? (verse 2b)

    d. What historical record is David drawing on in verse 3?

    e. What is it that amazes David about God as expressed in verses 3–4?

    f. In what way is man made "a little lower than the angels"? (verse 5a)

    g. Describe the privileged position of the angels in Isaiah 6:1–3.

    h. How has God crowned man with "glory and honor"? (verse 5b–8)

    i. What do you think it means for the animal kingdom to be put under man's feet? (verses 6–8)

    j. What should man's relationship be to the animal kingdom? How much "glory and honor" do you feel is being reflected by man's stewardship of the creation and animal kingdom?

    k. Summarize the message of Psalm 8. Why does David think God's name is so excellent "in all the earth"? (verses 1, 9)

2. Read Psalm 19:1–14.

    a. What are the two sources of wonder for David in this psalm? (verses 1–6 and 7–11)

    b. How do you think the "heavens declare the glory of God"? (verse 1)

    c. What is the tendency when something special is available 24 hours a day? (verse 2)

    d. Why is cynicism about creation a real possibility? Instead of recognizing God as the source of creation, what do many people cite as the source?

    e. Compare verses 3–4 with Paul's statement in Romans 1:19–20.

    f. How many peoples of the world have evidence available to them of the glory of God? (verses 3–4)

    g. Summarize the "human" characteristics by which David describes the sun. (verses 4b–6)

    h. Instead of viewing the Word of God as a "book," how does David seem to regard it? (verses 7–11)

    i. Describe what the Word of God is able to do for the person who embraces it:

        verse 7a

        verse 7b

        verse 8a

verse 8b

verse 11

j. In light of the greatness of God's Word, what is David's concern? (verses 12–14)

3. How amazed are you at the greatness of God's creation and the power of God's Word?

a. What can a Christian do to keep from taking God for granted in these two areas?

b. What is the most wonderful thing to you about creation and about God's Word?

DID YOU KNOW?

More and more scientists are beginning to stand in awe and wonder at the complexity and design found in creation—both in nature and the human body. Their observations and conclusions are leading them to reject evolution as an explanation for life. Instead, they are convinced that life on our planet is a result of intelligent design. The Intelligent Design movement is not a biblical or Christian movement (though all Christian scientists hold to intelligent design). Many scientists who believe in intelligent design do not recognize the God of the Bible as the "designer," but they believe evolution no longer can serve as an adequate explanation for the origins of life. The mysteries and miracles of life are so profound that more and more scientists are standing in awe of "whoever" created it. That's definitely a step in the right direction.

THE SACRIFICE OF WORSHIP

Genesis 22

In this lesson we discover that worship is always costly.

OUTLINE

Some people think sacrifice means going to church in the rain. But worship in Scripture conveys a different kind of cost; one that the worshiper bears personally. What we are willing to sacrifice is an indicator of the value we place on the object of our worship.

   I.   **Worship Recognizes That God Has Spoken**

  II.   **Worship Responds to What God Has Said**

 III.   **Worship Requires the Best We Have to Offer**

 IV.   **Worship Retreats to Be Alone With God**

  V.   **Worship Rejoices the Heart of God**

 VI.   **Worship Results in Blessing**

IN PREPARATION FOR THIS LESSON, BE SURE TO READ CHAPTERS SIX AND SEVEN IN THE BOOK, *My Heart's Desire.*

There is a law in the interpretation of Scripture which is called "the law of first mention." Basically it says that wherever you find a doctrine, word, or theme mentioned in the Bible for the first time, that passage can be understood to set the tone for understanding it throughout all of the Bible. The first mention of "worship" in the Bible is found in Genesis 22:5: "And Abraham said to his young men, 'Stay here with the donkey; the lad and I will go yonder and worship, and we will come back to you.'"

This comes in the most extraordinary setting, as Abraham is going to bring his own son to God in sacrifice. God calls that worship. It is the supreme act of worship which God expects from all of us. As we review this familiar story, there are a number of things it teaches us about worship.

WORSHIP RECOGNIZES THAT GOD HAS SPOKEN

In verses 1 and 2 we read, "Now it came to pass after these things that God tested Abraham, and said to him, 'Abraham!' And he said, 'Here I am.' Then He said, 'Take now your son, your only son Isaac, whom you love, and go to the land of Moriah, and offer him there as a burnt offering on one of the mountains of which I shall tell you.'"

As we've already seen earlier in this book, worship is a command from God. It is not an option for the believer. Here we see God in direct communication with Abraham, and He is not only telling Abraham to worship, He is telling him where to worship, and how he is to worship. This experience that Abraham is about to undergo is not something he thought up. This is God's idea. Understand that point: Worship is God's idea. It is not something your pastor has decided to do in order to get from the beginning of the service to the message. Worship is the idea born in the heart of God. It is His very passion.

If you take Abraham's obedience out of this story, what you have is not worship. You have premeditated murder. If Abraham is simply going to the mountain to kill his son, there is nothing godly about it. Child sacrifice is the most heinous act recorded in the Old Testament. But in response to an almighty God who has instructed Abraham in the act of worship, it becomes holy ground to all who understand worship. Remember, the worship of God and the work of God are always guided by the Word of God. Worship recognizes that God has spoken.

WORSHIP RESPONDS TO WHAT GOD HAS SAID

Notice verse 3: "So Abraham rose early in the morning and saddled his donkey, and took two of his young men with him, and Isaac his son; and he split the wood for the burnt offering, and arose and went to the place of which God had told him."

Too often when we tell these stories, we get caught up in the Old Testament setting and miss the impact of the action. If God directly communicated to me one day and said, "David, I want you to take your oldest son to a mountain, and there I want you to kill him in obedience and sacrifice to Me," what do you think I would do? I would probably call all my pastor friends to see if maybe I'm not misinterpreting this message. I'd gather them around and say, "You know, this doesn't really make any sense to me. I can't believe God would ask me to do this." I would probably tell the Lord I needed two or three weeks to pray about it.

But notice what Abraham did. He got up early the next morning to be obedient to God. There was no argument. There was no negotiating back and forth between Abraham and God. The fact that it did not make sense to him did not keep him from being obedient to what God had said. God clearly told him the way he was to worship and Abraham obeyed without any question. And note, too, that the record is clear that God honored and blessed him because of his obedience.

I've got a book on my shelf by Robert E. Webber entitled *Worship Is a Verb*. Basically what the book says is that worship is not a feeling, a thought process, or an emotion that comes over us. Worship is an activity we are involved in as a response to what God has asked of His people. Worship is an action that God wants you and me to make a part of our lives. Worship is not passive, but participative. If you attend a worship service and just watch everybody else, you haven't worshiped. You have been a spectator while others have worshiped! This is difficult for those of us who grew up watching the performance take place on the platform, watching others worship God, and wondering why we left with an empty feeling. Worship demands the involvement of your heart, mind, and energy. Worship demands a response on your part.

When God told Abraham, "I want you to go to the mountain and sacrifice your son," Abraham obeyed. He got up, he saddled his donkey, he took two young men, he prepared the wood, he went to the mountain—all of those are action words that tell us what Abraham did in response to God's Word. Abraham teaches us that worship responds to what God has said.

WORSHIP REQUIRES THE BEST WE HAVE TO OFFER

"Take now your son, your only son Isaac, whom you love, and . . . offer him there as a burnt offering." Friends, worship is not a cheap thing. God asked Abraham to offer his most prized possession —his own son. This boy meant everything to Abraham. This was the son in whom all the blessings and promises of God were to be fulfilled. Yet here is God saying, "This is how much your worship is going to cost you. Take your only son and offer him to Me."

Someone has suggested that in order for Abraham to obey, he had to surrender his intellect to God. After all, God had said, "In Isaac shall all of the promises be fulfilled." Abraham and Sarah had waited until they were almost 100 years old before Isaac had finally come, and God had been promising Abraham that He was going to bless him through his posterity. Now in old age he finally had a son. Isaac was a wonderful young man, and Abraham could see all the promises of God coming true through him. Yet God says, "Take the son that I promised you up to a mountain and kill him." Abraham must have thought, "Lord, I don't understand. This doesn't make sense! First You tell me that my future is wrapped up in Isaac, now You tell me to go and kill my future." It isn't until you get to the Book of Hebrews that you find out how Abraham put it all together. It says in Hebrews 11 that when Abraham was sorting this out, it finally came to him that the only way God could keep His promise was to raise the slain Isaac from the dead. You talk about faith! Abraham had to come to God in his worship and say, "I don't understand this, but I know this is what You've asked me to do, so I will sacrifice my intellect to You."

Abraham also had to sacrifice his emotions, since he deeply loved his son and would not want to cause him any pain. And he had to sacrifice his will to God, by obeying even when he did not want to. Until Abraham took his first step toward Mount Moriah, he had not begun to worship God. He surrendered his intellect, emotion, and will in order to obey God. Our culture has made worship easy and frivolous, but Abraham understood that worship is tough and demanding.

Generations later, King David came to the very spot where Abraham had attempted to sacrifice his son. The Bible tells us that David wanted to build a place where God could be worshiped;

a great temple where God would be honored and glorified. King David had been struck with this thought after realizing he was living in a beautiful house while the Ark of the Covenant was sitting in a tent. He determined to build a house for God and one day went in search of the perfect temple ground. The Scriptures say he wound up at the threshing floor of Araunah. David, thinking this the perfect spot for God's temple, offered to buy the property. Araunah, knowing it was for God, offered to simply give it to David. "No you won't!" David replied in 2 Samuel 24:24. "Nor will I offer burnt offerings to the Lord my God with that which costs me nothing." David understood that worship requires sacrifice, and he was not going to allow the temple of the Lord to be built cheaply.

After David died, his son Solomon built the most unbelievable temple to God on that very spot—the spot where Abraham offered his son Isaac to the Lord. They say Solomon's temple was the most magnificent building ever constructed to the honor and glory of God. This place became the focal point of what true worship is: giving God all that we have.

WORSHIP RETREATS TO BE ALONE WITH GOD

Notice verse 5 of Genesis 22: "And Abraham said to his young men, 'Stay here with the donkey; the lad and I will go yonder and worship, and we will come back to you.'" Why couldn't the others come? Why didn't everyone get to share in that great moment of worship? Because it was a sacred moment. Worship is a personal response to God, so even when it occurs in a group setting, the impact of worship relies on your personal response to God. Abraham didn't need anything to worship God except Isaac, the wood, and himself. He left behind everything that was extraneous. Together, he and Isaac climbed the mountain. There they worshiped God.

If we really are going to enter worship, we have to move away from all the things that get in our path. It's hard to worship in freeway traffic. It's hard to worship in the confusion of a shopping mall. It can be hard to worship in a church when everything is rushed, when there are a dozen activities, when there are two dozen announcements, and when our minds are on the baggage of the past week. We need to get away where we can put it all behind us and be alone with God. That can be a tough task in our information age. We have so much information to process that our minds get cluttered with bits and pieces of junk, and it takes a concerted effort on our part to set it all aside and prepare our hearts and minds to focus solely on God. That's why Abraham went quietly up the mountain with his son to worship.

WORSHIP REJOICES THE HEART OF GOD

In the rest of Genesis 22 you get the story of what happened on the mountain: how Abraham tied up his son, prepared to sacrifice him, and was stopped by an angel. I've often thought it would be wonderful to compare the face of Abraham on the way up that mountain and his countenance on his way down. Here is an old man, trudging up Mount Moriah with his son Isaac, who is carrying the wood, by his side. Fully aware of what God has asked him to do, his head must have hung and the tears must have welled in his eyes. He was fully ready to obey, but that would not have stopped his emotion. He probably took his time going up that mountain, preparing the altar, and binding his son. In your mind's eye you can see that aged patriarch ready his knife, then at the last moment have his hand stayed by the angel. Isaac was set free, but in his heart Abraham had already killed him. In that moment it became clear that there was nothing on earth more important to Abraham than God.

Now, can you imagine the trip down the mountain? I don't know if one-hundred-year-old men can dance, but I'm sure Abraham went down that mountain considerably faster than he went up. He had faced the most serious test of his life and proven himself faithful. He had felt the pleasure of Almighty God, who was well pleased by Abraham's obedience.

WORSHIP RESULTS IN BLESSING

This worship, which rejoiced the heart of God, also resulted in blessing for Abraham. Verses 17–18 tell us that God promised to bless him and multiply his family as the stars of heaven. "Your descendants shall possess the gate of their enemies. In your seed all the nations of the earth shall be blessed, because you have obeyed My voice."

The Bible says that when we honor God, God honors us. God will not be debtor to any man. You cannot out-give God. When you give Him your worship, He will shower blessings back upon you. But you must offer God everything. If you have not come to love Him with all of your heart, soul, mind, and strength, your worship will be empty. We need to cultivate the worship of God that was so significantly a part of Abraham. We need to offer God everything we have, everything we are. We need to come before Him and say, "Lord, there is not anything in my life that I love more than I love You." It is indeed a costly thing to worship God.

1. Read 2 Samuel 24:15–25.

   a. In what situation does David find himself in this passage? (verse 17)

   b. What was David instructed to do in light of his sin? (verse 18)

   c. What does David intend to do to quell the plague that has come upon the people? (verse 21)

   d. What did Araunah, the owner of the threshing floor, offer to David? (verse 22–23)

   e. What was David's response? (verse 24)

   f. Why was it important to David not to worship the Lord in a way that cost him nothing?

   g. With what is worship connected in Romans 12:1?

h. David sacrificed 50 shekels for a place to worship God. What is the believer called upon to sacrifice? (Romans 12:1)

2. Read Genesis 22:1–5.

   a. What was Abraham commanded by God to do? (verse 2)

   b. When they got to the mountain, what did Abraham tell the servants he was going to the mountain to do? (verse 5)

3. Why is personal sacrifice such a frequent component of worship in the Bible?

   a. How might one worship God without sacrifice?

   b. What is the ultimate sacrifice that was made which allows us to worship God?

   c. Who made that sacrifice so we would not have to?

   d. How does Christ being a sacrifice in death shed light on our responsibility to worship God by being a "living sacrifice"?

4. Read Daniel 3:1, 4–6, 12–18.

   a. What were the three Hebrew youths required to do in Babylon? (verse 5)

   b. What sacrifice would they be required to make in order to reserve their worship for God alone? (verse 6)

   c. Which did they value more highly—the purity of their worship or preserving their lives? (verses 16–18)

5. Read Matthew 26:69–75.

   a. While not a setting of worship specifically, what choice was Peter faced with?

   b. What was the price, or sacrifice, he decided not to make?

   c. What aspect of "worship" was at stake? (e.g., giving God proper homage and respect)

   d. What do you think you would have done in Peter's place?

6. What sacrifices, on a personal or corporate level, do you make in order to worship God?

a. What connection do you see between the prerequisite for sacrifice and the enthusiasm for worship (or lack of it) in the modern-day church?

b. How does the presence or absence of sacrifice affect the intensity of worship in the modern-day church?

DID YOU KNOW?

Worship is not defined in Scripture. Instead, we have a "semantic range" of words which provides descriptions of what people do when they are "worshiping." There is *proskuneo*, made up of two words, *pros* (toward) and *kuneo* (to kiss) which is used of acts of homage or worship (Matthew 4:10). *Sebomai* means to revere (Matthew 15:9), and *sebazomai* means to honor religiously (Romans 1:25). *Latreuo* means to serve or render religious acts of service (Philippians 3:3), while *eusebeo* means to act piously towards (Acts 17:23). Worship is more than just praise—it is acts which convey honor, reverence, and submission.

THE ENDLESS SONG OF WORSHIP

Selected Scriptures

*In this lesson we learn that musical praise is
at the heart of worship.*

OUTLINE

Ever wonder why Madison Avenue uses jingles and songs to sell products to the American consumer? It's because the human mind remembers words and melodies more easily than plain speech. That God-given ability finds its chief application in worship.

I. **Music and Old Testament Life**
    A. The Song of Worship at the Red Sea
    B. The Song of Worship by Deborah
    C. The Song of Worship for the Ark
    D. The Song of Worship at Solomon's Coronation
    E. The Song of Worship for Solomon's Temple
    F. The Song of Worship for the Rebuilt Walls
    G. The Song of Worship for the Rebuilt Temple

II. **Principles of Old Testament Worship**
    A. Worship Is Our Response to God
    B. Worship Is Reflective of Our Spiritual Life
    C. Worship Is a Release of the Whole Person to God
    D. Worship Is a Responsibility of Every Christian

IN PREPARATION FOR THIS LESSON, BE SURE TO READ CHAPTER EIGHT
IN THE BOOK, *My Heart's Desire.*

The Bible contains almost 600 references to people singing praises to God. Of the Bible's 66 books, 44 contain references to music. The Book of Psalms, with its 150 chapters, was once a Jewish hymnbook. There is more said in Scripture about singing than about prayer.

Singing is a unique expression of the image of God in man. Only man can communicate with organized language through the sounds of pitch, duration, and harmony. No other created being can sing like man, who was created by God as an instrument of praise. Christianity is the only one of the world's religions that is truly a singing religion. Music began at creation when "the morning stars sang together, and all the sons of God shouted for joy" (Job 38:7). That song has continued throughout the years, punctuated by great outbursts of heaven's praise like the angels' announcement on the hills outside Bethlehem. It is music that will occupy us in eternity. In heaven we will sing, "You are worthy, O Lord, to receive glory and honor and power; for You created all things, and by Your will they exist and were created" (Revelation 4:11). Heaven is the ultimate homeland of music.

One of the reasons God has blessed music is because music is such an effective teacher. It instills in our minds truths that we might never remember otherwise. Most of us can still remember biblical concepts we learned through Sunday school: *Jesus Loves Me, For God So Loved the World, Jesus Loves the Little Children.* Music teaches and trains, and it does so with a power that speaks not only to the mind but also to the heart. That's why those songs of childhood remain with us throughout life, long after other textbook matters have faded without a trace.

F. Olin Stockwell, a missionary in China who was imprisoned by the Communists, said that the training and indoctrination of young people in China was marked by singing. Each night the new cadres would learn catchy tunes with words that rang with communist ideology, singing themselves into communism.[1] Music is a powerful teaching tool. Just look at the place music held in Old Testament life.

MUSIC AND OLD TESTAMENT LIFE

The Song of Worship at the Red Sea

There was a song of worship after the Israelites had passed through the Red Sea on dry ground (Exodus 15:1–21). The first formal song recorded in Scripture came at a great moment of victory in the life of God's people. You know the story: The nation of Israel was fleeing Egypt, chased by Pharaoh's army, and got trapped by the Red Sea. But the Lord parted the waters and marched them through on dry ground. The Egyptians chasing after them were drowned when God allowed the waters to come crashing back onto them. Safe on the other side, Moses sat and penned a song about God's deliverance of His people. You can find it in Exodus 15:1–21. "Then Moses and the children of Israel sang this song to the Lord, and spoke, saying: 'I will sing to the Lord, for He has triumphed gloriously! The horse and its rider He has thrown into the sea!'"

The Song of Worship by Deborah

There was a song of worship when Deborah led the Israelites in victory over Jabin, king of Canaan (Judges 5). The first female songwriter in Scripture, Deborah was a judge over Israel. She went to war against King Jabin and won a miraculous victory. Afterwards, she wrote a song for the nation of Israel to sing together. The song is recorded in Judges 5, and the refrain goes: "Thus let all Your enemies perish, O Lord! But let those who love Him be like the sun when it comes out in full strength." She led the people of God as they sang and worshiped the Lord for His great deliverance.

The Song of Worship for the Ark

There was a song of worship when David brought the ark back to Jerusalem and had it enshrined there (1 Chronicles 15:16, 27–28; 16:4–7). This was a time when David learned about the working of God. He had tried and failed to bring the ark back once, only to have someone die by reaching out to touch it. Incensed, David abandoned the ark for a time. Later, after hearing that the home where it was residing was experiencing a special blessing from God, David decided to reclaim the ark the proper way. The Bible records that he appointed certain ones "to be the singers accompanied by instruments of music, stringed instruments, harps, and cymbals, by raising the voice with resounding joy" (verse 16). Verses 27 and 28 add, ". . . and Chenaniah the music master with the singers . . . with shouting and with the sound of the horn, with trumpets and with cymbals, making music with stringed instruments and harps" went before the ark. David even appointed certain Levites to produce music for this occasion to "thank, and to praise the Lord" (1 Chronicles 16:4). Then he wrote a lengthy psalm to commemorate God's faithfulness, recorded in 1 Chronicles 16:8–36, and gave it to Asaph, the music leader, to orchestrate as a fitting tribute to the ark's return to Jerusalem.

The Song of Worship at Solomon's Coronation

There was a song of worship at the coronation of King Solomon (1 Kings 1:39–40). On the day he was crowned King of Israel, we read, "Zadok the priest took a horn of oil . . . and anointed Solomon. And they blew the horn, and all the people said, 'Long live King Solomon!'And all the people went up after him; and the people played the flutes and rejoiced with great joy, so that the earth seemed to split with their sound." The earth shook with the sound of the rejoicing of God's people, there was so much noise and excitement.

The Song of Worship for Solomon's Temple

There was a song of worship when Solomon dedicated the temple of the Lord with a 4,000 voice choir (1 Chronicles 23:5; 2 Chronicles 5:11–14). Imagine a four thousand voice choir—with a four thousand piece accompaniment! There were actually 24 choirs, made up of 150 voices each, spread throughout Israel. Each choir would sing in the temple two weeks per year, except during the feasts when all the choirs would join together. There were also 288 master music leaders who trained singers for worship. This all helped make music the very center of Jewish faith and brought everyone to a place of praise. At the dedication all the singers and musicians joined together in praise. It was so awesome that the Scripture says the visible presence of the glory of God visited the people that day in the form of a cloud. The cloud, which was inside the temple, was so bright the priests who were doing the ministry could no longer see what they were doing. What an incredible time of worship!

The Song of Worship for the Rebuilt Walls

There was a song of worship when Nehemiah dedicated the rebuilt walls of the city of Jerusalem (Nehemiah 12:27). "At the dedication of the wall of Jerusalem they sought out the Levites in all their places, to bring them to Jerusalem to celebrate the dedication with gladness, both with thanksgivings and singing, with cymbals and stringed instruments and harps." It is interesting to note that spiritual revival is always associated with music. If you look at history, the two always have been together.

There was a song of worship during the revival led by Ezra after the wall was completed (Nehemiah 12:45–47). "Both the singers and the gatekeepers kept the charge of their God and . . . all Israel gave the portions for the singers and the gatekeepers, a portion for each day." Here again we see music associated with spiritual revival. D. L. Moody once observed that "music and song have not only accompanied all scriptural revivals, but are essential in deepening one's spiritual life. Singing does at least as much as preaching to impress the Word of God upon people's minds. Ever since God first called me, the importance of praise expressed in song has grown upon me."

The Song of Worship for the Rebuilt Temple

There was a song of worship when the temple was rebuilt and rededicated under Zerubbabel (Ezra 2:41, 65; 3:10–12). When Zerubbabel came back with the people of God to rebuild the temple that had been destroyed, they had barely gotten the foundation in place and they got so excited they decided to have a worship service. "When the builders laid the foundation of the temple of the Lord, the priests stood in their apparel with trumpets, and the Levites, the sons of Asaph, with cymbals, to praise the Lord, according to the ordinance of David king of Israel. And they sang responsively, praising and giving thanks to the Lord: 'For He is good, for His mercy endures forever toward Israel.'" Now, there were still some old men around who remembered the glory of Solomon's temple. They had gone through the anguish and pain of seeing that temple destroyed, and now they saw it coming alive again. When they finished the foundation, these men were so overcome with joy that the Bible says they wept aloud. There were old men weeping aloud and young men shouting for joy to the Lord so that you could not discern which was which. It was all offered up to God as one great presentation of praise and worship.

There was a song of worship when Jehoshaphat led his people against Moab and Ammon (2 Chronicles 20:21–28). The Bible says that Jehoshaphat "appointed those who should sing to the Lord, and who should praise the beauty of holiness, as they went out before the army and were saying: 'Praise the Lord' . . . [and] when they began to sing and to praise, the Lord set ambushes against the people of Ammon, Moab, and Mount Seir, who had come against Judah; and they were defeated." God blessed them with victory because He was pleased by the worship of His people.

PRINCIPLES OF OLD TESTAMENT WORSHIP

Of course there are many other songs in the Bible—songs telling of David's exploits, songs sung at the deaths of Saul and Jonathan, and songs praising the goodness of God. All of this emphasis on music leads us to several principles we can glean from Israel's worship.

Worship Is Our Response to God

In more than a hundred passages, the Scriptures describe the worshiper as "approaching" God. God said the tabernacle was the place "I will meet you and speak to you, there also I will meet with the Israelites" (Exodus 29:42–43 NIV). No one thought of coming to worship to receive anything, they came to give something back to God, to worship Him for all that He meant to them. In the process of meeting the need of God to be worshiped we find fulfillment. When you are singing, you are singing for God. He is the sole audience in a worship service. Perhaps we need to remember that the church is a place where we rendezvous with God to bow before Him. As the psalmist said, "I will praise the name of God with a song, and will magnify Him with thanksgiving. This also shall please the Lord" (Psalm 69:30–31).

Worship Is Reflective of Our Spiritual Life

We say much about ourselves by our singing. Music is the barometer of the church's spiritual life. When Israel abandoned God, their song became sad. When they remained faithful to Him, their worship was full of joy. The singing in churches today reveals the same truth. Worship is vibrant when the joy of the Lord inhabits the hearts of people. Music reflects our walk with the Lord.

Worship Is a Release of the Whole Person to God

Music is not just sounds that come from our mouths. Jewish worship included bowing, kneeling, prostrating, clapping, shouting, and lifting eyes and hands to the Lord. Instead of sitting in pews, the people were physically involved in worship. Worship is more than just sitting and listening, it involves a release of the whole person before God.

Worship Is a Responsibility of Every Christian

There were no non-worshipers in Israel. Everyone worshiped. The leaders led the entire body in worship, and everyone participated. As a Christian, you are now a New Testament priest. You have a responsibility to worship God. Even if you can't carry a tune, you are to be worshiping Him with enthusiasm. In the words of Paul, "I will sing with the spirit, and I will also sing with the understanding" (1 Corinthians 14:15).

Note

1. Quoted in Kenneth W. Osbeck, *The Endless Song* (Grand Rapids, MI: Kregel, 1987), 18.

1. Read Exodus 15:1–18.

   a. What is the theme of verses 1–3?

   b. What do verses 4–10 accomplish?

   c. Verses 11–12?

   d. Verses 13–17?

   e. Verse 18?

   f. What is the difference in tense (time orientation) between verses 4–10 and 13–17? Which section looks back and which looks forward?

   g. Therefore, Moses worships God for who He_____, what He has_____ , and what He will_____ in the future.

2. In the same vein as Moses' song . . .

   a. List some things God has done for you personally in the past:

   b. Now list some attributes or characteristics of God which those actions suggest:

   c. Finally, what are some things in the future that you should be able to trust God for based on who He is and what He has done in the past?

   d. Using the evidence of "attributes" and "actions" in Moses' song, write a simple definition of worship of God:

3. Read Psalm 150:1–6.

   a. Where are the two commanded locations for worshiping God? (verse 1)

   b. What does it mean to praise God "in His mighty firmament"?

c. For what two things is God to be praised and worshiped? (verse 2)

d. List the instruments with which praise is to be offered to God: (verses 3–5)

4. Read 1 Chronicles 15:16–29.

   a. What is your overall impression of the "trouble" David went to in preparing for proper praise and worship?

   b. In what spirit was the ark to be accompanied into Jerusalem? (verse 25)

   c. What was sacrificed by the Levites?

   d. How did David and the others prepare themselves for this event of worship? (verse 27)

e. Based on verse 28, describe in your own words what the scene must have been like that day:

f. How do you reconcile the appearance this verse gives with what Paul says about worship in 1 Corinthians 14:40?

g. What do you think is meant by the phrase "decently and in order"?

DID YOU KNOW?

The most primitive song recorded in the Bible is the song of Lamech (Genesis 4:23–24). Sadly, his song is not in praise or defense of God but of himself. As a descendant of the ungodly Cain, Lamech's boasting about his own actions and self-justification is consistent with his ancestor. Jesus was obviously familiar with this earliest song, since He plays off of it in teaching about forgiveness. Whereas Lamech boasted that he would be avenged "seventy-sevenfold" for his killing of a man, Jesus taught his disciples they were to forgive "seventy times seven" times when wronged (Matthew 18:22).

THE SONG CONTINUES

Ephesians 5:18–19; Colossians 3:16

In this lesson we learn why singing is a God-intended means of praise and worship.

OUTLINE

Instead of great singing, some Christians claim just to be making a "joyful noise" unto the Lord. Since God is more concerned with the heart than the art, that's okay. But every believer should use the gift of melody and music to worship God.

   I.   **Singing Is the Result of Being Filled With the Spirit of God**

  II.   **Singing Is the Result of Being Indwelt by the Word of God**

 III.   **Singing Is a Reciprocal Experience**

  IV.   **Singing Is a Response From the Heart**

   V.   **Singing Is a Richly Diverse Experience**

  VI.   **Singing Shows Reverence to the Lord**

IN PREPARATION FOR THIS LESSON, BE SURE TO READ CHAPTER NINE
IN THE BOOK, *My Heart's Desire.*

One of the most excellent vehicles for the presentation of our worship to God is music. Time and time again we see people in the Bible praising God in song. The angels sang praises to God at the birth of Jesus. Jesus sang a hymn to God after the last supper. Paul and Silas sang a hymn of praise to God while jailed for sharing their faith. Again and again in Scripture we are encouraged to sing praises to God.

Ron Allen, in his book on worship, said, "Singing for those redeemed by the grace of God should not be an obligation. . . . It seems totally inconsistent to be a joyful believer and a non-singer."[1] When you become a Christian, you become a singer. Even if you can't carry a tune, you are called to lift the name of the Lord in song. God is more concerned about your heart than your art. Consider the principles of singing we can glean from the New Testament.

SINGING IS THE RESULT OF BEING FILLED WITH THE SPIRIT OF GOD

Ephesians 5:18–19 says, "And do not be drunk with wine, in which is dissipation; but be filled with the Spirit, speaking to one another in psalms and hymns and spiritual songs, singing and making melody in your heart to the Lord." You know, I've heard some strange messages about what happens to a person when they are filled with the Spirit. What the Word of God says is that we begin to sing! We begin to admonish one another with psalms and hymns and spiritual songs. Singing the true song of worship is born out of the fact that God's Holy Spirit has come to live within us. There is a whole new dimension to our lives because the Holy Spirit is alive and well in our hearts. Martin Luther once said, "The devil hates music because he can't stand gaiety. Satan can smirk but he cannot laugh; he can sneer but he cannot sing."

Have you noticed the negativity going on in our world today? Our culture used to enjoy positive songs about life, like the old one from *Oklahoma!* "O what a beautiful morning, O what a beautiful day, I've got a beautiful feeling, everything's going my way." If you have a day like that, you just want to sing. Now most of what you hear on the radio is negative and depressing. But the difference in spiritual music is that even when everything is not going your way, the dynamic of the Holy Spirit is still in you and putting a song in your heart. What other group of people do you know who sings worship to God at funerals? When my mother passed away, we sang hymns at the memorial service. There was hurt in our hearts, but joy in our souls because we knew where she was. The Christian who has the Holy Spirit has the dimension of the supernatural in his life that makes it possible for him to look beyond his immediate circumstances and still be able to sing. Singing with the Spirit is the supernatural dimension of what we have in Christ. The Holy Spirit changes everything from the inside out, and singing is the natural result.

SINGING IS THE RESULT OF BEING INDWELT BY THE WORD OF GOD

Paul wrote these words to the Colossians: "Let the word of Christ dwell in you richly in all wisdom, teaching and admonishing one another in psalms and hymns and spiritual songs, singing with grace in your hearts to the Lord" (3:16). Note the subtle change in this verse compared with the previous verse. Paul tells the Ephesians that if they are filled with the Spirit, they will sing songs. But he tells the Colossians that if the Word of God dwells in them, they will sing songs. Brothers and sisters in Christ, there are only two things without which no one can become a Christian. One is the Spirit of God and the other is the Word of God. No one has ever become a Christian without those two things cooperating together in his or her life.

Once we become Christians, the Bible says the Spirit of God comes to live within us, and the Word of God begins to dwell in us richly. The inevitable result is that we want to sing. That is why all of the great hymns and songs that have made a lasting impression on us have had a direct tie to the Word of God. Many times it has simply been a songwriter finding a melody or rhythm to fit a line of Scripture that has created a beautiful song of praise to our God. The more we are indwelt by the Word of God, the more we want to sing His praises.

SINGING IS A RECIPROCAL EXPERIENCE

Notice that in Ephesians 5 and Colossians 3 our singing is to ourselves. Does that sound strange? We worship God by singing to ourselves and to one another psalms, hymns, and spiritual songs. It is a way to bring praise and glory to God.

During the Middle Ages church people were not allowed to sing. There was a church council that convened, and their reasoning was that if an individual believer does not have the ability nor the privilege of personal interpretation of the Scriptures, neither should he be allowed to sing the songs of the church. There were small groups in each church that performed whatever music there was. The average church attendee sitting in the pew was not allowed to sing at all. Can you imagine what that would be like? Well, along came Martin Luther to fix the problem. Luther wrote, "Let God speak directly to his people through the Scriptures, and let his people respond with grateful songs of praise." Luther wanted the Bible and the ability to sing given back to the layman. He went on to write 37 hymns to help us worship, many of which we still sing today.

If you had lived during Old Testament days, you would not have been able to offer up praise to God individually as we do today. In your quiet time you could worship God in your own spiritual way, but not at all like we do as Christians. Spiritual worship in the Old Testament was offered to the Lord through the priests and Levites who were specialists in worship. But when Jesus Christ came and died on the cross, He opened up the way for us into the Holy of Holies and we became priests. Every believer is a priest, according to the Bible. And as priests we have individual responsibility and authority before God. That's why Peter says, "You also, as living stones, are being built up a spiritual house, a holy priesthood, to offer up spiritual sacrifices acceptable to God through Jesus Christ" (1 Peter 2:5). And Hebrews 13:15 tells us that one of the spiritual sacrifices is "the fruit of our lips," the sacrifice of praise. As a believer, you have instant access before God and are responsible as His priest to offer sacrifices to Him in singing and praise. So as you sing to others of His glory, you offer a sacrifice as a priest and it brings glory to Him. Thus singing is a reciprocal experience.

SINGING IS A RESPONSE FROM THE HEART

Colossians 3 speaks of "singing with grace in your hearts." Ephesians 5 mentions "singing in your heart." You know, I cannot find any place in Scripture where it tells us how to sing. But there are many passages that tell us what ought to be going on in our hearts while we are singing because spiritual worship is not so much a state of the art as it is a state of the heart. Worship God from your heart.

There is a story told of a leper who was isolated in a colony, held captive by her disease. Though there were few on earth that knew or cared about this poor woman, there was a missionary who came to visit her. One day he led her to the Lord, and God put a song in her heart. By this time the disease had ravaged her body and taken away all the mechanism necessary for singing. I have seen film footage of this young lady, singing to the Lord with a sound that is almost reprehensible as it squeaks out of the brokenness of her body. But I dare say it must have been some of the most beautiful music heaven ever heard because it came from her heart.

God wants to hear music being played through the strings of our hearts. Sing to the Lord, and let God be honored and glorified through your music. God looks at the heart, not the outward appearance. God listens to the melody of our hearts, not just the notes from our lips. Let your singing be a response from your heart unto God.

SINGING IS A RICHLY DIVERSE EXPERIENCE

The Scripture says, "Singing to the Lord with psalms and hymns and spiritual songs." There is a great controversy in the church today over what style of music we are to use in worshiping the Lord. But these verses clearly show that in the very earliest days of the church there was not any one particular style. There has always been diversity among God's people. They sang some psalms, some hymns, and some spiritual songs.

The psalms Paul mentions were the Old Testament songs of Israel, which we know today as the Book of Psalms. There were also other songs from Old Testament literature. In the New Testament we read how Jesus and His disciples used the psalms at the Feast of Tabernacles and at the Passover Supper. The psalms were majestic, beautiful presentations of Old Testament texts, set to music. The psalms remain with us today as the classics in music for all of us to enjoy. Many of the greatest composers have taken those passages and richly endowed them with music to bring honor and glory to God. We will never want to be rid of the psalms that we sing.

We are also to praise the Lord with hymns. For first century Christians, hymns were newer religious expressions that communicated the teachings of Christ. They taught New Testament doctrines, and they were applied to the Christian life and faith. There are many people who believe that in the New Testament itself a number of hymns are included. For example, Paul's testimony about Christ's humility in Philippians 2:5–11 is probably a hymn, as is John's writing in Revelation 4:11. Of course, most of the hymns with which we are familiar have been written relatively recently. Reading the words of a Fanny Crosby or a Charles Wesley hymn is both uplifting and educational.

The "spiritual songs" category is the part that usually creates the most controversy. The words we translate "spiritual songs" literally mean "ode to a breath." It is something that spontaneously explodes out of one's spirit. New Testament worship services were much less formal than ours are today. Apparently someone might stand up right in the middle of the service and sing a solo. When they were done, someone else might get up to read Scripture, and then another might pop up and begin to pray. Corporate worship was far more diverse than what we have today. New melodies might be created, with truths sung to popular tunes. Spiritual songs were the forerunners of the beautiful worship choruses and praise music we have today. These songs often don't have a long life; they seem to appeal to their generation and then are replaced by newer styles of music. Hymns that seem formal to us might surprise us by their origins. Martin Luther and others actually used melodies of common life in their day and added the words of God's truth.

In the New Testament we are given the freedom to be different and diverse. A good worship service will weld together various pieces to create one beautiful praise offering to God. The key issue is that God's people worship Him through a variety of music. When we come together and minister to one another, we minister unto the Lord.

SINGING SHOWS REVERENCE TO THE LORD

Paul talks of "singing . . . to the Lord." Worship may minister to those who are together, but it has as its goal sacrifice to the Lord. We are in His presence when we worship. We take ourselves before Him, offer our sacrifice of praise, and are transformed by Him. God loves to take a miserable heart and replace it with the joy and peace that comes from knowing Him. He will take away the depression and despair and replace it with a song. And as that individual, changed by the Holy Spirit, worships the Lord by singing His praises, our great God is glorified even more.

Note

1. Ronald Allen, *Worship—Rediscovering the Missing Jewel* (Portland, OR: Multnomah Press, 1982), 154.

APPLICATION

1. Read Colossians 3:16.

   a. What instructional purpose did musical worship play in the early church?

   b. How can songs "teach" and "admonish"?

   c. What relationship did Paul imply between the word of Christ dwelling in the believer and the singing of spiritual songs?

   d. What would be the difference between a person singing "with grace" and without grace in his heart?

   e. Which book of the Bible is a collection of songs?

   f. What does it mean to "sing with grace in your hearts to the Lord"? (NIV or NASB translations)

2. Read Ephesians 5:18–19.

   a. Besides the Word of God (Colossians 3:16), what else does a worshiper need to be filled with? (verse 18)

b. What do you think were (are) the differences between psalms, hymns, and spiritual songs?

c. Where does singing originate? (verses 18–19)

d. How might worship differ depending on whether one is filled with the Spirit or not?

e. What is Paul suggesting by using "filled with wine" as a point of contrast for "filled with the Spirit"? (Also Acts 2:11–17)

f. What does Paul mean by "speaking to one another" with songs? (verse 19; Colossians 3:16)

g. Are you familiar with churches which use hymns and spiritual songs as a teaching medium? How do they do it?

h. How often do you use singing in your own personal worship time with the Lord?

3. Record your insights about the "new songs" which are sung in Scripture (reason, accompaniment, audience, etc.).

   a. Psalm 33:3

   b. Psalm 40:3

   c. Psalm 96:1

   d. Psalm 98:1

   e. Psalm 144:9

   f. Psalm 149:1

   g. Isaiah 42:10

   h. Revelation 5:9

   i. Revelation 14:3

j. What does "new song" suggest about the ongoing process of praise and worship in the church? How often should "new songs" be written?

4. Have you ever written a song of praise to the Lord? Ask God to give you a "new song" to Him based on your experiences of His acts and attributes.

DID YOU KNOW?

First Kings 4:32 tells us that King Solomon composed 1,005 songs. The greatest of his songs goes by the name "Song of Songs"— its title in the Old Testament (Song of Songs 1:1; "God of gods and Lord of lords" [Deuteronomy 10:17] and "King of kings" [1 Timothy 6:15]). While not a worship song to or about God, it nonetheless is a testament to the central and powerful place of song in the biblical cultures. Because it is a beautiful and passionate song about married love, some have suggested it fulfills a second role in Scripture as a picture of the love relationship between Christ (the groom) and the church (the bride) (Ephesians 5:22–33).

WORSHIP AT HOME AND ON THE ROAD

Selected Scriptures

In this lesson we learn how to worship God anywhere, anytime.

OUTLINE

Having a building in which to worship each Sunday has many practical benefits. If there is a downside, it is thinking that worship is restricted to only that place and time. God has made every believer in Christ a temple in which He lives, a place where worship takes place continually.

I. **A Parable**

II. **A Principle**

III. **A Possibility: Three Metaphors**
   A. Your Body: A House
   B. Your Body: A Temple
   C. Your Body: A Tent

IV. **A Presence**

V. **A Prescription**
   A. First, please avoid using that mental picture of the religious fanatic
   B. Second, think about what God would be likely to do through you in relation to other people
   C. Third, rid yourself of those ideas that your life would become burdensome and joyless if you lived out your faith

VI. **A Program**
   A. Every Day Worship in Solitude
   B. Every Day Worship in Service
   C. Every Day Worship in Struggles
   D. Every Day Worship in Sacrifice

IN PREPARATION FOR THIS LESSON, BE SURE TO READ CHAPTERS THREE AND FOUR IN THE BOOK, *My Heart's Desire.*

A PARABLE

Once there was a magnificent castle in which lived a wise and generous king. The monarch loved his subjects greatly, but few of them ever ventured near the gleaming castle. The king was lonely for his subjects, feeling like a parent whose children had turned their backs on him, never to return. He decided that if his people would not come to him, he must go to them. Instructing his attendants to remain behind, he ventured alone to the town square. Naturally, the town folk were shocked to see their king walking among them unattended, and a hush fell over them. They watched nervously as the king knelt down to play a game with two small children. As more children gathered around, the adults began to draw near as well.

By the time the sun was setting, a great love and bond was formed between them. He promised them a way to remember and experience his love for them whenever they wanted. He pulled from his robe a beautiful flute and handed it to a young girl. "Like this flute, each of you will find a beautiful musical instrument when you return to your homes. Whenever you play upon your instruments, I will come to you. Your instruments will play the Praise Song of the King, and the music will bring me to you wherever you may be. The music will always remind you of the companionship we have formed today."

The little girl began to blow on her flute, and the most beautiful melody anyone had ever heard came forth. For the first time, the people saw their king for who he really was. The melody told who their king was, and therefore it told them who they were. When the king left, the people hurried to their homes where they discovered the instruments the king had promised. From that day forth they played their instruments daily and, somehow, the king came to each one and spent time with them. Whether they played alone or together, the king came; and the melody grew deeper and richer with each playing of it. The king lived in the music, and the music lived in the people.

Some say the music of the king can still be heard today. Have you heard it? Have you tried to hear it?

A PRINCIPLE

God is our King who has come to us because we would not come to Him. In the person of Christ He walked among us and showed us what He was truly like. He invited us to begin a relationship with Him that would provide access to His presence at any time. The great passage of Paul's in Philippians 2:5–8 summarizes how God our King came to earth to walk among us.

But even before Bethlehem, God had made His home among humans in a different and unique way: in the worship of His people. Just as the king in the parable gave his people an instrument by which they might be in his presence at any time, so God has given us an instrument by which we dwell in His presence as well—and that instrument is worship. David, the singer of Israel, wrote of God, "But thou art holy, O thou that inhabitest the praises of Israel" (Psalm 22:3 KJV). Another Bible version translates it this way: "The praises of Israel are your throne" (NCV).

This truth is the answer to a great mystery surrounding praise. Why does healing come with praise? Why does brokenness and repentance come with praise? Why do so many transformations occur in the presence of praise and worship? The answer is because, while God is everywhere present, He manifests Himself among His people in their praise of Him. As a person who travels frequently, I have learned to be at home almost anywhere. And yet there is no substitute for returning to my real home, my own true family. Such is the way of God when He dwells where He is most at home—in the praise of His people.

C. S. Lewis wrote, after stumbling with the concept of worship as a new Christian, "I did not see that it is in the process of being worshipped that God communicates His presence to men." It is not the only way, of course. But people seem to encounter God more directly in worship than in any other way. A bowed head, a humbled heart, and an attentive spirit form a doorway to heaven for the faithful worshiper. When we worship we experience what the villagers in the parable did. We discover the innocence of children with musical instruments who simply blow their flutes or pluck the strings of their harps. In an amazing way, God comes to us and spends time with us and attends to us as we attend to His worship. Just as a human father settles into his most comfortable chair in the presence of his loving children, so God settles in and dwells in the praises of His people. Wherever I am—when I'm in a hotel traveling far from home and church—I can still use the instrument of praise to call upon the presence of the Lord.

Sadly, the word "worship" is, like "love," a word that has been overused in our culture to the point that it has lost its true meaning. A sacred concept has become profane, used to describe our feelings about anything and everything. We need to look into Scripture and remind ourselves of the true meaning of worship—its relation to sacrifice, to music, to a place of worship, to our spiritual lifestyle. By recapturing the essence of worship, we will be blowing the dust off the beautiful instrument the King has given us, one that has been set aside or misused, the instrument that brings God into our presence and us into His.

A Possibility: Three Metaphors

Your Body: A House

Robert Boyd Munger wrote a beautiful little book called *My Heart, Christ's Home*. In it he pictures our life like a house in which Christ wants to live. The story unfolds as Jesus is invited in and walks through the house making changes in the various rooms. The rooms, of course, represent the various dimensions of our lives. It is a compelling metaphor for how we need to give over our whole life to the worship of God. But there is an even stronger metaphor we can examine.

Your Body: A Temple

Paul wrote two letters to the church in Corinth—a group I like to think of as "Sunday only" Christians. They gathered on the Lord's Day to worship, but none of their worship seemed to carry over into their daily lives. All kinds of immoral and immature activities characterized the church at Corinth. Paul rebuked the church sharply, especially for their sexual sins (1 Corinthians 6:19–20). His message was that God wants all your life—body, soul, and spirit. He intends for the Christian's body to be a temple for His own holy presence. Just as you wouldn't engage in immoral activities in the temple in Jerusalem, so we shouldn't in the temple which is our body (2 Corinthians 6:16). Jesus compared His own body to the temple (Matthew 26:61) and now that He lives in us, we are the temple of God (Ephesians 2:21).

Your Body: A Tent

The final metaphor Paul uses is that we are a tent, a temporary home (2 Corinthians 5:1, 4). Peter makes use of the same picture in 2 Peter 1:13–14. A tent is perishable, designed for people on the move which is certainly characteristic of the Christian. This earth is not our home; we're just passing through on the way to our heavenly home (Philippians 3:20; Hebrews 11:13).

A temple is a holy dwelling, a place for the very presence of God. There was a time when the temple of God was a tent, the Tabernacle of the Old Testament, before it was built permanently in Jerusalem. The laws of God were enshrined in the ark of the covenant and traveled with the people of God. The law was a symbol of God's presence as they journeyed in the wilderness. This picture helps us to see worship as a lifestyle in the same way that Paul does in the New Testament (1 Corinthians 6:20; 15:58; Ephesians 5:20; 6:18; Philippians 4:4; Colossians 4:12; 1 Thessalonians 5:16–17; 2 Thessalonians 3:16).

When we put together all the New Testament references to worship, prayer, remembering God, thanking God—and doing it all "without ceasing" (Romans 1:9; 1 Thessalonians 1:3; 2:13; 5:17; 2 Timothy 1:3)—we see the Christian life as one of unbroken communion with God. I suggest we move beyond Robert Boyd Munger's helpful image of a house as the dwelling of God to a modern image of a temple on wheels! We don't leave Jesus at home when we go to the office or market. Instead, He goes with us everywhere we go. He is with us, and we are worshiping Him, in every moment of our lives.

A PRESENCE

The missing elements in the use of the house as a metaphor for the dwelling of God are wonder, awe, and holiness. A house invokes a warm and homey image, but a temple suggests a dwelling built for the worship of a mighty God. The Corinthians were living reverence-impaired lives. They had no sense of the awesome holiness of God, and the offense their sins caused Him. Granted, the temples of our bodies are ragged and torn compared to the granite shrines of old—but they invoke the image of holiness nonetheless when we think of them as temples. We need to think of ourselves as the mobile presence of God—a place where the law is enshrined, where God dwells, where others gather to experience God's presence, a resource of worship and praise.

A PRESCRIPTION

Does this idea of being a temple scare you away? It might if you're thinking of the religious fanatics you encounter in airports and on street comers who are more offensive by their intrusions into our lives than they are spiritually attractive. Three correctives can help us keep the right perspective on what it means to be a dwelling place of God.

First, please avoid using that mental picture of the religious fanatic

Satan is ready to put images of religious fanaticism into your mind when you think of living a life wholly dedicated to God. Why? Because the greatest threat to his program is people who carry the living God around with them and manifest Him wherever they go. Instead of thinking of religious fanatics, think of a Christian leader you admire for his or her gracious, yet committed, stand for Christ. You'll be reminded that it is possible to take Christ with you wherever you go.

Second, think about what God would be likely to do through you in relation to other people

Would God be eager for you to walk into a crowd, or into your office, and begin rudely spouting religious rhetoric, antagonizing people and driving them away from Christ and the Gospel? Or, would God empower you to serve and counsel people at their point of need, coming alongside them as a loving and supportive friend? People can be attracted to you in the same way they were attracted to Jesus if He is with you wherever you go.

Third, rid yourself of those ideas that your life would become burdensome and joyless if you lived out your faith

I'm not sure how people arrive at this reasoning, but they sometimes think, "If I start ministering to people and inviting them to my church . . . I could become overwhelmed, with no time for myself. My life is complicated enough!" Do you not think God is able to meet your needs and bless you as you manifest His life wherever you go? Take your spiritual life on the road and give God a chance to prove Himself.

What would this kind of life look like, and how do you develop it?

A Program
Every Day Worship in Solitude

Anything that is a lifestyle is something we do every day. If living in the presence of God is going to be your lifestyle, you must worship alone with God every day. Are you surprised, even disappointed, that I've suggested something so basic and simple?

A lack of complicated secrets is not our problem in the spiritual life —it's a failure to be faithful in the basics. Meeting alone with God in the morning has advantages: It sets the tone for your day; God can show you things in prayer or the Word to prepare you for what He knows is coming; and you run less risk of procrastinating and perhaps not spending time alone with God at all.

Every Day Worship in Service

The same Greek word in the New Testament can be translated "worship" or "serve." When we serve others in the name of Christ, we are actually worshiping God. Worship in the Old Testament was law based, while worship in the New Testament is life based. Jesus told the woman of Samaria that a time was coming "and now is" when geography would have nothing to do with worship (John 4:21–23). Rather, spirit and truth would be the determinants for true worship. Therefore, you can go anywhere, empowered by the spirit and truth, and serve others as a lifestyle of worship.

Every Day Worship in Struggles

Anyone who allows worship to be disrupted by difficulties will find themselves not worshiping very consistently. Life is filled with struggles, and they present some of the best opportunities for us to worship God as an act of our will rather than our feelings. We can worship God in struggles because of Romans 8:28—we know God causes all things to work together for good for those who love Him. Even when facing death, as David and Jesus did (Psalm 22:1; Matthew 27:46), we can worship God since we know He has the final victory (1 Corinthians 15:54).

Every Day Worship in Sacrifice

The apostle Paul exhorts us to present our bodies as a living sacrifice to God, which is a "reasonable service"—or a proper response of worship in light of the "mercies of God" (Romans 12:1). All of life is a sacrifice. If we are going to obey God instead of this world or the dictates of our flesh, we will give up something; we will sacrifice. The important thing is the idea within the moment— "Lord, I praise and exalt Your name, and I give this thing to You. Take my life and let it be consecrated, Lord, to Thee."

The truth is that when your life becomes a temple, a home for Jesus, you begin to see His face in the faces of all those who surround you. You begin to treat them as you would treat Him. You begin to realize that all ground is holy ground, because God is there. You begin to see every situation as a potential act of worship, a time to magnify the name of the Lord.

1. Read Philippians 2:5–11.

   a. In what way was Christ God when He came to earth?

   b. In what way did He set aside His deity and identify with mankind?

   c. What did He do with His reputation as God? (verse 7)

   d. What "form" did He take? (verse 7)

   e. If you had passed Jesus in the marketplace of Jerusalem, how would His appearance have differed from other men? (verse 7; see also Isaiah 53:2)

   f. In what ways did Jesus have to humble Himself while on earth? (verse 8)

   g. Where did His obedience to God lead Him? (verse 8)

   h. What did God do in response to Jesus' obedience? (verses 9–11)

   i. What was Paul's purpose in relating this information? (verse 5)

   j. What do you learn from Jesus' example about your own

      Reputation?

      Humility?

      Possible cost for worshiping God?

2. Read Deuteronomy 6:4–9; 11:18–21.

   a. How does verse 5 present a picture of the person who worships God with his whole life?

   b. What question was Jesus answering when He quoted this verse? (Matthew 22:36–37)

   c. If one keeps the "greatest law," how would that impact his lifestyle?

   d. How many of our daily sins can be traced back to a failure to keep this first and greatest law?

   e. What does verse 7 suggest about how this law (and all of God's laws) should be "carried" about in the life of the believer?

   f. Opposites in the Hebrew language ("lie down . . . rise up"; verse 7) implied everything in between as well. In what situations, therefore, is the believer exempt from loving God with all his being?

   g. What do you think is the implication for daily living in verse 8?

   h. Where should the law of God be carried by the believer? (verse 9)

   i. What is the difference between keeping God's Word in your mind and in your heart and soul? (Deuteronomy 11:18)

j. What difference might you notice in the lifestyle of a person who stored up God's Word mentally but not "soulishly"?

3. For you, what are the practical implications of Paul referring to your body as . . .

   a. a tent?

   b. a temple?

   c. a temporary dwelling?

   d. a sacred dwelling place of God?

DID YOU KNOW?

The oldest form of worship in the Old Testament is family worship. Even before Israel became a nation, it was already a worshiping family—the family of Abraham, Isaac, and Jacob. It wasn't until after the exodus, when the children of Israel became a nation, that the national forms of worship were established. The rise of the synagogue made possible a more continuous form of congregational worship and offered new opportunities for instruction, but the family was the core of the worship experience.

WORSHIP IN ETERNITY

Revelation 4:1–11

In this lesson we get a glimpse of what worship in heaven will be like.

OUTLINE

We know more about what won't be in heaven (prayer, pain, problems, and plagues) than what will. We do know at least one thing that heaven will be full of: worship. The throne of God and the worship of the Lamb will be our central focus for all eternity.

I. **The Throne of Heaven**

II. **The Praise of Heaven**

III. **The Perspective of Heaven**

IN PREPARATION FOR THIS LESSON, BE SURE TO READ CHAPTER ONE
IN THE BOOK, *My Heart's Desire*.

V Raymond Edman, formerly the chancellor of Wheaton College, was a very devout man. He wrote numerous books which express his great love for the Lord, and I have learned much from him. In 1967 he was preaching in the college chapel on worship. He told his students that several years earlier he had had the opportunity to meet the king of Ethiopia. In order to meet the king, there was a strict protocol to which he had to attend. There were a number of items which had to be done in order that he might present himself properly to that earthly king. Dr. Edman used that illustration to remind the young people that when they came to chapel each day at Wheaton College, they were coming into the presence of the King of kings. He urged them to understand what it meant to worship the Lord. While he was offering the student body several suggestions for making chapel more worshipful, Dr. Edman suddenly collapsed to the floor and entered the very presence of the King.[1]

As I reflect on that event, I remember several commentators noted that, in their opinion, Dr. Edman would have one of the easiest transitions into the presence of God of anyone they had ever known. He so loved and worshiped God during his lifetime that entering into eternal worship would not be much of a shock to his system. He would just flow right into the worship of God because he had spent all of his life doing that very thing.

Wouldn't it be great if our worship approached that of heaven's worship? Wouldn't you love to experience worship that was similar to that experienced by the saints in glory? In our worship services we have three integral parts: The praising of God, the praying to God, and the preaching about God. It is a strange and interesting thing that when we get to heaven only one of those three elements will survive.

As far as we know, there is no prayer in heaven because there is no need to pray. We are in the presence of Almighty God and we are living in light of His every good wish for us, so there would be no need to pray in terms of supplication. Nor would there be a need for intercession, because if we have failed to intercede for loved ones on earth, it will be too late in heaven. There is not going to be any preaching in heaven either, because the Bible says that we will know Him even as we are known. We will have perfect knowledge in terms of understanding the things of God.

Praising is the only one of the three that will remain in our worship before the Lord. The Bible says that we are going to spend eternity in praise and worship of Almighty God. If that is true, then praise and worship must be a very high priority with the Lord. It behooves us, as His people, to take seriously the biblical instruction that we have already been given and to continue to grow in our ability to worship and praise God. What we are learning to do in our short time on earth, we will spend an eternity doing in heaven.

In the fourth chapter of the Book of Revelation we are given just a little glimpse into our eternal worship and praise. It is interesting that the chapter begins by telling us about a door being opened into heaven. John, exiled to the island of Patmos for preaching the Gospel, "looked, and behold, a door standing open in heaven" (verse 1). Apparently John was given the opportunity to look through that door into the very throne room of glory, and get a glimpse of eternal praise. In the process of seeing that, it had a profound effect upon the apostle. If we understand what he saw, and if we comprehend what God wants us to know in light of what John saw, it will have a profound effect on our worship. What John sees on the other side of that door is massive worship taking place. It is a marvelous picture. If we are to see it, we will have to rely on the Spirit of God to assist us in understanding and appreciating the scene.

THE THRONE OF HEAVEN

The key word in this chapter is the word "throne." That word is found 46 times in the Book of Revelation, and 14 times in chapter four. The word "throne" speaks of sovereignty, reign, and control. When you read in Revelation about the throne of God, it is a reminder that while chaotic events are taking place on earth, we should never lose sight of the fact that God remains on His throne in heaven. To many of us it may appear that no one is in control of events on earth, but John reveals that God is seated on His throne, reigning and ruling. The throne of God is neither abandoned nor vacant.

As John sees that throne, he tries to describe his vision. He has a very difficult job, because the primary focus of the throne is God Himself. The Bible says that no one can see God and live, and John does not offer a description of God. He does offer a symbolic representation to try to help us understand Him. The symbolism can give us a great sense of the nature and personhood of God.

John says that when he looked, "a throne [was] set in heaven, and One sat on the throne. And He who sat there was like a jasper and a sardius stone" (verses 2–3). The jasper we would today call a diamond; a beautiful, many faceted stone that sparkled and glittered in the light. John said that as he looked upon that throne all he could comprehend was the brilliance of a diamond. The diamond was accompanied by a sardius or camellian stone, which is the complement to our ruby. Around the throne there was a rainbow that looked like an emerald. John, looking at the throne, saw diamond, ruby, and emerald—the beauty of God as best he could describe it in human writing. As he gazed at the majesty and beauty of his eternal Creator, all he could comprehend was that it was like a brilliant diamond, ruby, and emerald on the throne.

John also noticed that there were 24 seats around the throne, occupied by 24 elders. Many folks have argued about the identity of the elders, but Scripture identifies them as representatives of the church of the Living God. Revelation 5:8–10 tells of those 24 elders singing praise to the Lord: "When He had taken the scroll, the four living creatures and the twenty-four elders fell down before the Lamb, each having a harp, and golden bowls full of incense, which are the prayers of the saints. And they sang a new song, saying: 'You are worthy to take the scroll, and to open its seals; for You were slain, and have redeemed us to God by Your blood out of every tribe and tongue and people and nation, and have made us kings and priests to our God; and we shall reign on the earth.'"

So John saw God on His throne, the emerald rainbow encircling the throne, the glassy sea surrounding it, and the 24 elders representing the church. The Scripture goes on to say that John saw four living beasts representing all that is mightiest and grandest in creation. They had six wings and many eyes, and Revelation speaks of their incessant activities, continually crying out God's holiness. It was an amazing scene to John—one that was quite overwhelming.

THE PRAISE OF HEAVEN

As he watched that magnificent scene, John was allowed to listen to what was about to happen. "Whenever the living creatures give glory and honor and thanks to Him who sits on the throne, who lives forever and ever, the twenty-four elders fall down before Him who sits on the throne and worship Him who lives forever and ever, and cast their crowns before the throne, saying: 'You are worthy, O Lord, to receive glory and honor and power; for You created all things, and by Your will they exist and were created'" (Revelation 4:9–11).

John was allowed to see heavenly worship. He wrote about the magnificence of that occasion which helps us have a glimpse of what our eternal occupation will be. We are going to be part of that great worship experience where forever we bring honor and glory to our God. It won't be something we are made to do, it will be something that grows out of the very nature of who we are in Christ. We will find worship to be the most joyous experience we have ever known. Worship is to ascribe to One what is His by virtue of His nature. In Revelation 4 the Lord is given glory and honor and power because He is the creator of all things, and all things were created for His pleasure. All the earth sings praise to the Lord because He made it. And with that scene in mind, there is a great lesson about worship that can revolutionize our corporate and private worship.

THE PERSPECTIVE OF HEAVEN

John was allowed to experience two realities. Isolated on Patmos, separated from friends, and worried about the persecution of the church by Roman emperor Domitian, John was facing discouragement. Yet in a moment of time he is ushered out of that reality through an open door into heaven. He sees the Lord, seated on a throne, the picture of sovereign control. He sees the elders bowing down and worshiping. He sees the beauty and majesty of heaven. God gave John this experience not only so that he could write about it, but to encourage his heart. Here he is, discouraged and depressed, and suddenly he is allowed to enter into the control room of the universe to see God's purpose and plan for all mankind.

The purpose is that we should worship the Lord, adore Him, and give honor and glory to His name. You and I are constantly bombarded with the reality of this world. Television, radio, and newspapers are incessantly getting us to focus on this world and on our present reality. Yet this reality is in contrast to the unseen reality of heaven. Christians often live as though eternal things are somehow less real. According to Scripture, they are not less real. That which is eternal is real. That which we know here on earth is temporal. The eternal God sits in judgment on that which is temporal. When John was ushered into the presence of God, everything that was going on in his life was immediately brought into perspective by the eternal. This is one by-product of our worship that grabs my attention.

Many of us come to worship in difficult circumstances. Some reading this are out of work, struggling with their health, or experiencing emotional pain. It's easy to attend church and, in your heart, say, "I don't feel like worshiping God." Yet if you understand the dynamic of this principle, it is in those moments when you feel least like worshiping God that you must worship Him. In the process of elevating your praise to the Lord, you are lifted into the presence of God. God causes everything to make sense when you see it in light of His eternal sovereignty.

In the Lord's Prayer we find this kind of perspective. The Lord Jesus begins and ends with an eternal perspective: "Our Father, in heaven," and "For yours is the kingdom and the power and the glory forever" (Matthew 6:9, 13). If you start and end your prayers with an eternal perspective, you can pray your heart in the middle: "Give us this day our daily bread" (verse 11). That prayer will lift you out of the mire of your own situation and put you on solid ground. If you don't pray like that in your worship, you'll only feel more depressed than ever. We come first of all to bring honor and glory to the Lord, and in doing so we glimpse His mighty power. Then everything begins to make sense. That lifts the burden and gives control to God, and then we experience the joy of worshiping One greater than ourselves. As you learn to praise God better in your own private life, your church will begin to praise Him better corporately. In the act of worshiping God, we become healthy believers. Instead of being blown about by every wind of experience or circumstance, we see life from God's perspective and we can walk an even course.

Jesus is telling John, "I want you to know that things are not as they appear to be. I'm going to show you how things really are. I'm going to walk you into the throne room of heaven and show you genuine reality. Things are not out of control, Satan has not won, evil has not triumphed. Peek through the door and get a glimpse of reality. God is on His throne." That's what worship does for us. When we worship Him, it transforms who we are.

Note

1. Quoted by Leslie Flynn, *Worship: Together We Celebrate* (Wheaton, IL: Victor, 1983), 11.

1. Read Revelation 4:1–11.

   a. What was the first thing John saw when he was taken into heaven? (verse 2)

   b. Why is God described in terms of a rainbow and precious jewels? (verse 3)

   c. Who were those seated around the throne of God? (verse 4)

   d. What do these "elders" represent?

   e. What do the four living creatures do day and night without stopping? (verse 8)

   f. If you are a believer in Christ, what are your thoughts about witnessing this eternal worship service one day in heaven?

   g. How can 14 English words be repeated, without stopping, for all eternity without losing their meaning? (verse 8)

h. What is the longest you have ever spent in a time of uninterrupted praise of God?

i. What do the elders do, taking their cue from the living creatures? (verses 9–10)

j. What is the meaning of casting their crowns before God's throne? (verse 10)

k. What reason do they give for worshiping God? (verse 11)

l. If the elders represent the church, what does it appear the church's main purpose will be in heaven?

2. Read Luke 2:8–15.

a. From where did the angel come? (verse 9, 15)

b. Who is the angel personally representing? (verse 9)

c. What impression do the shepherds get of heaven's perspective on the birth of Christ? (verses 13–14)

d. Who do the angels praise and worship at this point in history? (verse 14)

e. Why do they not praise the newborn Savior at this time? (see Revelation 5:9)

f. Where do the angels go when their praise of God is finished? (verse 15)

g. What might we conclude that the hosts of heaven are most focused on?

3. Read Revelation 21:22–22:5.

a. Why is there no temple in the New Jerusalem? (verse 22)

b. Why is there no sun and moon? (Revelation 21:23; 22:5)

c. What will never enter the New Jerusalem? (Revelation 21:27)

d. What are the thrones of God and the Lamb the source of? (Revelation 22:1)

e. What will the saints of God be doing for eternity? (Revelation 22:3)

f. What will the saints see forever? (Revelation 22:4; 1 Corinthians 13:12)

4. How anxious are you to enter into the worship of heaven? What is the best way on earth to prepare for entering your heavenly home?

DID YOU KNOW?

Of the 175 occurrences of the English word "throne" in the Bible, fully one-fourth of them (42) occur in a single book—Revelation. It is fitting that the last book of the Bible—the book which wraps up history on earth and introduces us to heaven—should be filled with thrones. Scripture is the record of man attempting to establish his throne in place of God, and Revelation is where the contest reaches its climax. In the last days, most of the earth will worship the throne established by Satan for his representatives. But God prevails and establishes His throne for eternity. It is God's throne around which eternal worship will rightfully take place.

WORSHIPING THE LAMB

Revelation 5:1–14

In this lesson we discover how the ascended Christ is worshiped in heaven.

OUTLINE

The contrast between how Christ was reviled on earth and how He is revered in heaven is startling to say the least. One who went from being crucified on earth is now being magnified in heaven. The journey from cross to crown is the theme of heaven's choirs.

I. **He Is Worshiped Because of Who He Is**
   A. The Lion of the Tribe of Judah
   B. The Root of David
   C. The Lamb That Was Slain

II. **He Is Worshiped Because of Where He Is**

III. **He Is Worshiped Because of What He Does**
   A. Those Who Worship the Lord Are the Redeemed
   B. Those Who Worship the Lord Are the Angels
   C. The Whole Universe Worships the Lord

IN PREPARATION FOR THIS LESSON, BE SURE TO READ CHAPTER FOURTEEN
IN THE BOOK, *My Heart's Desire.*

In Revelation chapter five we are told that John, allowed a glimpse into heaven, sees the great God of the universe on His throne. In His hand is a book. It is a seven-sealed scroll, the title deed to the earth. This scroll will be unrolled throughout the rest of Revelation to unveil the outpouring of judgment and wrath on the earth. As each seal is broken, more of the scroll is unveiled until gradually we can read in detail the retaking of the earth by King Jesus. John, in his vision on the island of Patmos, sees that picture in heaven, the seven-sealed scroll in the hand of God the Father. But as all heaven waits, no one is found worthy of being able to open the scroll. John's eyes fill with tears because no one is worthy of saving the earth. Then an elder steps forward and tells John that there is One who is worthy to open the scroll, and he begins to describe Him. When that One is introduced, there is the most massive outpouring of praise in the history of the universe. It is a story so marvelous it is hard for us to describe it.

HE IS WORSHIPED BECAUSE OF WHO HE IS

He is the One described as the Lion of the Tribe of Judah, the Root of David, and the Lamb that was slain. Three names for the one person who is worthy to take the scroll.

The Lion of the Tribe of Judah

The Lion of the Tribe of Judah relates to the passage in Genesis 49 where Jacob, about to die, gathers his sons around him to bless each one. When he comes to his son Judah, he says, "Judah is a lion's whelp . . . The scepter shall not depart from Judah, nor a lawgiver from between his feet, until Shiloh comes; and to Him shall be the obedience of the people" (verses 9–10). That prophecy was clear to the people at the time: the Messiah would come from the line of Judah. If you study the genealogy of Jesus, you will find that is exactly the way He came. Jesus, described as the Lamb of God, is also the Lion who has all power and might, and who will come in majesty.

The Root of David

The second name given Him is "root of David." When Jesus walked this earth He was called "son of David," because He was a direct ancestor of King David. Yet here He is called the "root," as though He were both father and son. In His deity, Jesus was before David. He was David's ancestor because He existed before all things and created all things. Yet He was also David's progeny because He appeared on earth long after King David. Wrapped up in that eternal picture of God called "I Am," He is the root of David.

The Lamb That Was Slain

Finally, He is the Lamb that was slain. He is the One who is worthy to open the scroll because of His sacrifice for sin. There are four important lessons in this picture of Christ as the Lamb of God.

First, He is the Lamb who is standing. That is odd because slain lambs don't stand; they lie still on the ground. This slain Lamb stands. He was slain on the Cross, yet now He stands, resurrected.

Second, He is the Lamb who was slain. Much of our attention in heaven will be paid to the One who redeemed us. Did you know that when Christ appears in heaven, He will still bear the marks of our redemption in His body? The nail prints in His hands and the wound in His side will always be with Him, the Lamb that was slain. He paid the penalty for our sins that we deserved to pay, and we will rejoice throughout eternity every time we see the Lamb who bore our sins on the Cross. Worthy is the Lamb that was slain!

Third, He is the strong Lamb. The Scripture says He has seven horns, which refers to strength and authority. Seven is God's number of completeness, so He is a Lamb who is all powerful. He is not only the meek Lamb who is slain, but the strong Lamb who is in control, ready to bring judgment to the earth.

Fourth, He is a searching Lamb. He is described as having seven eyes, a way of saying that He sees all things. When we read about Him and understand who He is, we can begin to understand why all those who have a vision of Him fall down and worship Him. He is the focus of worship.

Notice that the Worthy One is both Lamb and Lion. He came as a Lamb to die for us. He will return as a Lion to rule the earth. As the Lamb, He is the Savior. As the Lion, He is the sovereign King. As the Lamb, He was judged. As the Lion, He will do the judging. As the Lamb, He was meek. As the Lion, He is majestic. In Revelation 5 we see Him standing, ready to return to this earth and wreak judgment upon those who have rejected Him.

HE IS WORSHIPED BECAUSE OF WHERE HE IS

Jesus is seen by John in heaven. All attention is on Him, the very center attraction of heaven. He is the focal point of all those gathered there, the One to whom every eye is looking. He is in the midst of the throne of God, worshiped by those surrounding it.

HE IS WORSHIPED BECAUSE OF WHAT HE DOES

Christ is about to reclaim authority over the earth. As soon as He takes the scroll, the weeping ends and the praising begins. The weeping is that of a creation looking to the redemption that is ours in God. So when the Lamb takes the scroll in His hand and is about to initiate the process of reclaiming the earth, weeping stops and worship begins. Three choruses of praise take place, one after the other. There is no other passage in Scripture where there is more magnificent, massive praise. This may be the greatest praise passage in all of God's Word. It is the focal point of all history, when all of the redeemed and all of the angels and all of the universe come before God to proclaim that He alone is worthy.

Those Who Worship the Lord Are the Redeemed

Note that those who worship the Lord are the redeemed. "The twenty-four elders fell down before the Lamb, each having a harp, and golden bowls full of incense, which are the prayers of the saints. And they sang a new song, saying: 'You are worthy to take the scroll, and to open its seals; for You were slain, and have redeemed us to God by Your blood out of every tribe and tongue and people and nation, and have made us kings and priests to our God; and we shall reign on the earth'" (Revelation 5:8–10).

Why is it that people today do not worship God? It can only be because they do not know Him. You cannot truly know God and not worship Him. To know Him—to understand the majesty and magnificence of His person—is to immediately fall down and worship Him. The barometer of our knowledge of God is our ability to worship Him. The more we know Him, the more we crave to worship Him. As these elders are gathered before the throne, they have come to see the One who is the reason for their very presence and, knowing Him, they fall down to worship Him.

In their hands are bowls containing the prayers of the saints. Did you know that God collects your prayers in a bottle? Maybe those prayers are simply the repeated theme the Lord taught His disciples: "Thy kingdom come, Thy will be done, on earth as it is in heaven." The prayers of the saints have ascended up to God, and now He is about ready to answer them and bring His kingdom to earth. So the saints of every nation and tongue and tribe praise Him by singing songs of praise because they have been redeemed.

Those Who Worship the Lord Are the Angels

It is also interesting to note that the angels worship God. Verses 11 and 12 state: "I heard the voice of many angels around the throne, the living creatures, and the elders; and the number of them was ten thousand times ten thousand, and thousands of thousands, saying with a loud voice: 'Worthy is the Lamb who was slain to receive power and riches and wisdom, and strength and honor and glory and blessing!'" Endless numbers of angels are gathered in the throne room of the glory of God and, after the redeemed have praised Him, the angels begin praising Him. Their worship is a bit different since the redeemed sing their praise directly to God, and the angels express their praise about God. There is no Scriptural evidence that the angels sing, perhaps because they have never experienced the joys or sorrows of this life. So their worship is different from ours, but they still enter into the praise of our great God.

The Whole Universe Worships the Lord

At the end of the fifth chapter, we read, "And every creature which is in heaven and on the earth and under the earth and such as are in the sea, and all that are in them, I heard saying: 'Blessing and honor and glory and power be to Him who sits on the throne, and to the Lamb, forever and ever!'" All of the earth praises God. What a magnificent scene this is with the whole universe bowing down before the Lamb that was slain.

There is really a growing crescendo of praise in the Book of Revelation. In 1:6 there is a twofold doxology: "to Him be glory and dominion." Then in 4:11 a threefold doxology: "You are worthy, O Lord, to receive glory and honor and power." By the time we come to 5:13, there is a fourfold doxology: "Blessing and honor and glory and power be to Him who sits on the throne." And in 7:12 there is a sevenfold, or perfect, doxology: "Blessing and glory and wisdom, thanksgiving and honor and power and might, be to our God forever and ever. Amen." The more people come to know Him, the more their praise and worship of Him grows until there is a perfect crescendo of praise that cannot be contained.

If you truly know God—if you have come to know Him in a progressive way in your Christian life, your heart and soul are just vibrating with worship for your great King. What we read in Revelation chapter 5 is just enough to give us a little taste of triumphant worship.

There is an old hymn that summarizes this worship:

'Tis the church triumphant singing,
"Worthy is the Lamb."
Heaven throughout with praises ringing,
"Worthy is the Lamb."
Thrones and powers before Him bending,
Incense sweet and voice ascending,
Swell the chorus never ending,
"Worthy is the Lamb."

Every kindred, tongue and nation,
"Worthy is the Lamb."
Join to sing the great salvation,
"Worthy is the Lamb."
Loud as mighty thunder roaring,
Floods of mighty waters pouring,
Prostrate at His feet adoring,
"Worthy is the Lamb."

Harps and songs forever sounding,
"Worthy is the Lamb."
Mighty grace for sin abounding,
"Worthy is the Lamb."
By His blood He dearly bought us,
Wandering from the fold He sought us,
And to glory faithfully brought us,
"Worthy is the Lamb"!

Sing with blessed anticipation,
"Worthy is the Lamb."
Through the vail and tribulation,
"Worthy is the Lamb."
Sweetest note all notes excelling,
On the theme forever dwelling,
Still untold though ever telling,
"Worthy is the Lamb"!

—Words by J. Kent

1. Read Revelation 5:6–14.

   a. Who is the focus of worship in John's next vision? (verse 6)

   b. What do the living creatures and elders do in His presence? (verse 8)

   c. Why did the creatures and elders speak their praise of God but sing their praise to the Lamb? (verses 8–10)

   d. Why do the creatures and the elders praise the Lamb? (verse 9)

   e. Who else joins in the praise in heaven? (verse 11)

   f. For what reason is the Lamb worthy to be praised in the angels' eyes? (verse 12)

   g. How does the climax of this vision fulfill the promise of Philippians 2:10–11?

2. Using the elders' new song as a model, write down four reasons why the Lamb is worthy to be praised by *you*:

   a.

   b.

   c.

   d.

3. Using the angels' song as a guide, write down four things the Lamb is worthy to receive from *you*—and why:

   a.

   b.

   c.

   d.

4. Read Isaiah 11:1–10.

   a. What is Jesus called in Revelation 5:5 in connection with David?

   b. Who was David's father? (Ruth 4:22; 1 Samuel 16:19)

   c. Why is the house of Jesse pictured by Isaiah as only a stump with roots? (verse 1)

   d. What does Isaiah say will come forth out of the stem (trunk) of Jesse? (verse 1)

   e. Who does this "branch" or "shoot" appear to be? (verses 2–5)

   f. If Jesus descends from David, why does the apostle John call him the "Root of David"? (Matthew 1:1; Revelation 5:5)

   g. How does Matthew 22:42–45 help answer the previous question?

5. Read 1 Chronicles 29:10–12.

   a. Compare the list of attributes mentioned by David in his farewell prayer to those ascribed to Christ and the Father in Revelation:

   1 Chron. 29:10–12   Rev. 4:9–11   Rev. 5:12   Rev. 5:13   Rev. 7:12

   b. When John ascribes the same attributes to the Lamb as to the Father, what is he saying about the deity of the Lamb?

DID YOU KNOW?

Of the 102 references to a "lamb" in the Bible, more than one-fourth of them occur in the Book of Revelation—all but one referring to Jesus Christ as the Lamb of God. The throne of God and the Lamb of God are two central themes in Revelation—both having to do with authority in heaven and on earth, and who will exercise it. The Lamb is pictured as having been slain on earth, resurrected, glorified in heaven, the avenger of those who take His name on earth, the coming judge of those who do not, and the recipient of praise and worship in heaven and earth forever.

THE WARFARE OF WORSHIP

2 Chronicles 17–20

*In this lesson we discover that worship
is a weapon of spiritual warfare.*

OUTLINE

The Christian life is an ongoing spiritual battle. When confusion, despair, temptation, and oppression are present, Satan may be the cause. Ironically, when worship seems least inviting or appropriate, that is when it is most needed as a weapon of spiritual warfare.

I. **An Old Testament Illustration**
    A. Crisis Number One
    B. Crisis Number Two

II. **Two Modern-Day Illustrations**

IN PREPARATION FOR THIS LESSON, BE SURE TO READ CHAPTERS TEN
AND ELEVEN IN THE BOOK, *My Heart's Desire.*

It was seven o'clock on a Friday evening in the city of San Francisco. Jerry Brandt, head of Action Evangelism, had scheduled an outdoor praise and prayer service in Union Square. It was to take place at eight and kick off a drive for the city's homeless. Jerry had filled out all the paperwork and had received permission to use the park, but as they were setting up he noticed a crowd of angry people gathering. "Who's in charge here?" a man from the crowd growled. "Well, I'm second in command," Jerry said. "Jesus Christ is in charge." The man ignored him. He didn't care about permits or permission, but simply barked, "We've got a thousand people on their way here, and as soon as they arrive we're taking this place over."

Jerry knew he had to say something, and fast. He felt the Lord impressing him with these words: "Let me tell you something. You're too late. Jesus has already taken over this square, and we're going to lift up His name tonight in this place." Then Jerry gathered his coworkers together and prayed for the rest of their people to show up as soon as possible.

One of the crew members read aloud Deuteronomy 28:7: "The Lord will cause your enemies who rise against you to be defeated before your face; they shall come out against you one way and flee before you seven ways." Then they began to sing praise choruses to God. It wasn't long before the promise was fulfilled. As Jerry and his friends worshiped the Lord, something dramatic happened. The marchers stopped in their tracks. They turned and headed away from Union Square as fast as they could, almost walking over each other to get away. They had heard the praise of God and wanted no part of it.

"Looking back on that night," Jerry recalls, "We realized God had delivered us and had used the power of praise to do it. Ever since that night, in our work ministering to people on the streets, we have discovered that praise and worship are the keys to our spiritual warfare."[1]

Some people see praise as witness, most see praise as worship. But few recognize praise as warfare. Yet the Bible makes it clear that praise and warfare go together. In fact, in Old Testament times there was really no difference between the two. If the community's worship was bad, so was their warfare. There are dozens of stories in Scripture, when God's people went out to battle and were soundly defeated because their worship was not right. The modern church has forgotten that God wants to use worship as an implement of warfare. If we do not lift up clean hands and have a clean heart, our ability to defeat the enemy is diminished. One author has said, "Satan is allergic to praise so that wherever there is massive, triumphant praise he is paralyzed, bound and banished." Mary Slessor, a missionary to Africa, said, "In the midst of all the demonic activity and all the pressures on my life, I have one little way to function: I sing the *Doxology* and dismiss the devil." Amy Carmichael adds, "I believe truly that Satan cannot endure praise and worship, so he slips out of the room while it is going on."

Worship as warfare is nothing new. Ignatius of Antioch, writing in 110 A.D., said this in his non-canonical Epistle to the Ephesians, "Take heed, then, often to come together to give thanks to God and show forth His praise, for when ye come frequently together in the same place, the powers of Satan are destroyed and his fiery darts urging to sin fall back ineffectual. For your concord and harmonious faith prove his destruction and literally torment his assistants."[2] You can render Satan inoperative by praising God! No wonder Paul and Silas sang and praised God at midnight in the Philippian jail. No wonder Jonah, laying in the belly of the whale, began to worship and give thanks to God. It was so contrary to the atmosphere that the whale couldn't stand it and vomited him up on the beach. Worship is powerful warfare.

AN OLD TESTAMENT ILLUSTRATION

The classic passage on worship and warfare occurs in 2 Chronicles 17–20.

Crisis Number One

The key player in the story is Jehoshaphat, king of Judah. He was one of the few good kings in that period, and while reigning over Judah he was challenged by the king over Israel, Ahab, one of the most wicked men who ever lived. Ahab and his wife, Jezebel, were a benchmark for evil in the Old Testament. They were the total opposite of Jehoshaphat, but a marriage was arranged to form an alliance between the two kings. Ahab brought Jehoshaphat to his kingdom, wined and dined him, and tried to talk him into going to war with him against another enemy.

Jehoshaphat knew better. He had been warned by a prophet, "Don't get involved in an unholy alliance with that wicked man. What do you, a man of God, have to do with a man who is unrighteous and unholy?" But because they were now related through marriage, Jehoshaphat was drawn into the relationship and off they went to war. It was a war that killed Ahab through one aimless bowman's shot, and left Jehoshaphat wondering why he had disobeyed God's counsel. Walking in his front door, who should be waiting for him but a preacher to confront him: "Then Jehoshaphat the king of Judah returned safely to his house in Jerusalem. And Jehu the son of Hanani the seer went out to meet him, and said to King Jehoshaphat, 'Should you help the wicked and love those who hate the Lord? Therefore the wrath of the Lord is upon you. Nevertheless good things are found in you, in that you have removed the wooden images from the land, and have prepared your heart to seek God'" (2 Chronicles 19:1-3). The rest of chapter 19 is a history of what happened after Jehoshaphat got a second chance to walk with the Lord.

Crisis Number Two

Soon, Jehoshaphat was given an opportunity to see what he had learned. Second Chronicles 20:1–3 tells us what occurred: "It happened after this that the people of Moab with the people of Ammon, and others with them besides the Ammonites, came to battle against Jehoshaphat. Then some came and told Jehoshaphat, saying, 'A great multitude is coming against you from beyond the sea, from Syria; and they are in Hazazon Tamar' (which is En Gedi). And Jehoshaphat feared, and set himself to seek the Lord, and proclaimed a fast throughout all Judah."

Now that is a good start. First, it is not wrong to be afraid. If Jehoshaphat had not been afraid in that situation, we would know there was something wrong with him. Fear is just a way of saying, "I don't have the resources myself." So, being afraid, he calls for a fast. The people came together and, according to the Scriptures, "from all the cities of Judah they came to seek the Lord"(verse 4).

Is seeking the Lord usually your last resort? Too many Christians live that way. Jehoshaphat learned that lesson through the bitter experience with Ahab. So he got his people together, and they sought the Lord. "Jehoshaphat stood in the assembly of Judah and Jerusalem, in the house of the Lord, before the new court, and said: 'O Lord God of our fathers, are You not God in heaven, and do You not rule over all the kingdoms of the nations, and in Your hand is there not power and might, so that no one is able to withstand You?'" (verses 5–6) Then he went on to praise God for who He is, what He has done, and what the king knows He can do. Then, in verse 10, he turns his praise into a very precise request: "'And now, here are the people of Ammon, Moab, and Mount Seir—whom You would not let Israel invade when they came out of the land of Egypt, but they turned from them and did not destroy them—here they are, rewarding us by coming to throw us out of Your possession which You have given us to inherit. O our God, will You not judge them? For we have no power against this great multitude that is coming against us; nor do we know what to do, but our eyes are upon You.' Now all Judah, with their little ones, their wives, and their children, stood before the Lord" (verse 10–13).

Notice the difference between crisis number one and crisis number two. In the first instance, Jehoshaphat used his own wisdom against the counsel of God and got into major trouble. In the second instance, he resorts to God and begins the interchange with a strong testimony of worship and praise. Now he has his people together, focused on the Lord, and he is about to decide how to go to war. What happens next is perhaps the strangest military experience of all time.

One of the prophets stands up and gives a little sermon. In effect he says, "Trust in the Lord and you will be successful. Listen to your prophets and you will be fine." So Jehoshaphat gathers them together and tells them, "We're going to war. Let's plan our strategy." The Scripture tells us the details: "Jehoshaphat bowed his head with his face to the ground, and all Judah and the inhabitants of Jerusalem bowed before the Lord, worshiping the Lord. Then the Levites . . . stood up to praise the Lord God of Israel with voices loud and high. So they rose early in the morning and went out into the Wilderness of Tekoa; and as they went out, Jehoshaphat stood and said, 'Hear me, O Judah and you inhabitants of Jerusalem: Believe in the Lord your God, and you shall be established; believe His prophets, and you shall prosper.' And when he had consulted with the people, he appointed those who should sing to the Lord, and who should praise the beauty of holiness, as they went out before the army and were saying, 'Praise the Lord, for His mercy endures forever.' Now when they began to sing and to praise, the Lord set ambushes against the people of Ammon, Moab, and Mount Seir, who had come against Judah; and they were defeated. For the people of Ammon and Moab stood up against the inhabitants of Mount Seir to utterly kill and destroy them. And when they had made an end of the inhabitants of Seir, they helped to destroy one another. So when Judah came to a place overlooking the wilderness, they looked toward the multitude; and there were their dead bodies, fallen on the earth. No one had escaped" (2 Chronicles 20:18–24).

Is that a strange tale or what? As the choirs of Judah sang praises to God, the enemy got confused and started to kill each other. Then when they finished killing each other, they killed themselves. So when Jehoshaphat's armies came to the place where they expected a giant army, all they saw were bodies on the ground. The Bible goes on to say that there was so much spoil among the dead armies it took days to bring it back. And after they got all the loot back to town, they had another praise and worship service to give God glory for what He had done through spiritual warfare.

You know, God won a major battle on behalf of His people through worship and praise. And since He inhabits the praises of His people, He could do the same work today. He goes forth to do mighty works when His people are anointed with praise and worship and they are willing to give Him the glory.

Two Modern-Day Illustrations

I know of a mission in Mambasa, Kenya, that played praise music over the loudspeakers at a rally. They could literally hear the demons screaming out loud in pain because of the praise that was lifted up to God. I have missionaries in my church who have told me that this often happens in the dark, Satan-dominated countries of the world.

Rich Hagens, a pastor in southeast Alabama, recognized that their large number of teen suicides was demonically led, so he organized a praise and worship service to confront the cults and Satan worshipers in town. They met them in a graveyard at midnight on Halloween, and Rick and his congregation simply sang songs and hymns of praise. The enemy was struck dumb. Those who came to taunt and jeer were transfixed by the worship of God, and the suicides stopped that very night.

Satan is alive and at work in our culture, and God has put us here to be a witness for His glory and grace. We need to learn how to use the tools the Lord has given us. We have the whole armor of God, and we are to stand and fight. Worship and praise are tools for spiritual warfare that we need to learn how to use. We need to know how to worship God continuously in private so that we can come together corporately and encourage one another to go forth into battle. I encourage you to make use of worship music as a pattern in your life. God will use worship to give you a power you never knew about. I also want to encourage you to pray continuously so that you are in regular communication with the heavenly Father.

Notes

1. Story adapted from Michael Coleman and Ed Linquist, *Come and Worship* (Old Tappan, NJ: Chosen Books, 1989), 80–83.
2. St. Ignatius of Loyola, *The Epistle to the Ephesians*, Chapter XIII, lines 93–94.

1. Read Exodus 17:8–16.

   a. What situation did the children of Israel find themselves in at Rephidim? (verse 8)

   b. What did Moses do in the natural realm to defeat the Amalekites? (verse 9)

   c. What did Moses do on the hill overlooking the battle? (verse 11)

   d. What did the raising of his hands signify?

   e. When Moses' hands grew tired, what did he do to continue his appeal to God in the midst of the battle? (verse 12)

   f. What was the outcome of the battle? (verse 13)

   g. What meaning did Moses attach to the altar he built there? (verse 16)

   h. What two things did Moses do to defeat the Amalekites?

i. How would you apply those two "weapons" to spiritual warfare today? (Is there often a "natural" as well as a "supernatural" element?)

j. What lesson(s) can you draw from Moses' weariness in appealing to the Lord?

k. And what lesson(s) can you draw from his appealing to Aaron and Hur to help him persevere in prayer and appealing to the Lord?

l. Is going before the Lord in worship and prayer one of the first, or last, things you do when experiencing spiritual attack?

m. Who do you have as friends who will join you in going before the Lord when seeking victory?

2. Read James 4:6–8a.

   a. Who does God oppose? (verse 6)

   b. And who does He give grace to? (verse 6)

c. If you are in a spiritual battle, do you want God opposing you, or the enemy?

d. What is the surest way to cause the devil to flee from you? (verse 7)

e. How effective will you be in resisting the devil apart from God?

f. Therefore, what is the prerequisite for resisting the devil? (verse 7a)

g. From what you have learned so far in this study on worship, what is the best way to demonstrate submission to God?

h. How can the devil attack someone who is continually worshiping and praising God?

i. What does God give to the humble to make them victorious? (verse 6)

j. To what degree can a proud person worship God?

k. Who is more likely to be attacked by Satan—a proud Christian or a humble Christian? Why?

3. What does Psalm 22:3–5 contribute to your understanding of the connection between worship and warfare?

DID YOU KNOW?

When Allied forces invaded Europe on D-Day, June 6, 1944, the second World War was essentially ended. While the surrender of the Axis forces did not occur until 1945, the presence of the Allied armies in Europe signaled their defeat. The battles that took place from D-Day until the end of the war were simply demonstrations of the fact that a superior power was in place. The spiritual life is like that. The events of Christ's crucifixion and resurrection signaled the defeat of Satan. The spiritual warfare we encounter until Christ returns is not for the purpose of defeating Satan. Rather it is the opportunity to demonstrate that the battle has already been won.

THE WISE WHYS OF WORSHIP

Habakkuk

In this lesson we learn that worship can fill the void of understanding in the darkest hours of life.

OUTLINE

Like quizzical two year-olds with their parents, we beseech God for answers when we don't understand life's events: "Why, God?" In truth, we need answers from God less than we need the God of all answers. And we find Him in the intimacy of worship.

I.   Habakkuk's "Whys"

II. Habakkuk's Wondering

III. Habakkuk's Worship

IN PREPARATION FOR THIS LESSON, BE SURE TO READ CHAPTERS TWELVE AND THIRTEEN IN THE BOOK, *My Heart's Desire.*

In Muskegon, Michigan, a Christian couple was looking forward to the birth of their fourth child. They already had three young daughters and had been told to expect a son this time. Filled with anticipation, the couple prayed that their children would grow to love God. One night, as the couple prepared for a walk after dinner, the husband received a phone call from a business associate. He told his wife to go on ahead, that he would catch up with her. But his phone call was extended and when he finally got away, he was unable to find her. He soon ran into a teenage boy and his father, searching for a deer the boy thought he had clipped with his fender. In a short time, they found he had not hit a deer, but had struck this young mother as she walked along the side of the road. Her neck was broken and her husband found her lying in the ditch, dead.

He was a godly man, a Christian husband, but there is nothing imaginable to encompass that man's tragedy and anguish that night. Yet my friends told me that the following Sunday that young father spoke to the congregation of God's glory. He gave thanks and praise to the Lord, and testified to the grace, mercy, and strength of the living God that sustained him during the most tragic hour of his life. I tear up thinking about that incident. Is there anything you can imagine that could so sustain a man, that in an hour like that he could stand in front of his peers and give glory to God? There is only one source I know that could do it—the Lord of Glory and King of kings, the God enthroned on high, who by His Spirit lives within the heart of every believer.

When our hearts face the imponderable, that is when we most need the Lord. When there are problems we cannot resolve, we may wonder if we are the only ones to ever question God. But we are not. The prophet Habakkuk was a man who questioned God. His book is a dialogue with God over the imponderables of life.

The Book of Habakkuk is a marvelous book. It is unique in that it was not written to give us addresses of a prophet to the people of his day. All of the other prophets recorded messages they preached to their people, but Habakkuk is not a message to the people of God. It is simply a dialogue between a prophet and God Himself. It is the record of the questioning and answering that goes on between a prophet and his God. It is literally a look behind the scenes at the heart of a prophet agonizing in his spirit over questions that seem to him to have no answers.

The Book of Habakkuk is the grandfather of the Reformation. In Habakkuk 2:4 you have for the first time the phrase, "The just shall live by his faith." Paul read Habakkuk; Martin Luther read Paul; and that, in short, is how we got the Reformation. It all leads back to the Book of Habakkuk.

One of the things that intrigues me as I come to understand the message of this great book is that the name Habakkuk literally means "to embrace." This is a wonderful picture of a man who, in the midst of unanswered questions, still was able to embrace the God he served. The book records the greatest turnaround in the shortest period of time of any in Scripture. Compare the spirit of the man in the first three verses to that of the last chapter and you will see the marvelous change that overcame the spirit of this man.

HABAKKUK'S "WHYS"

The prophet Habakkuk lived at a time when the people of God were straying far from the holy principles of Yahweh. His heart was broken by the sin of his people; and at the beginning of his letter he says, "The burden which the prophet Habakkuk saw. O Lord, how long shall I cry, and You will not hear? Even cry out to You, 'Violence!' and You will not save. Why do You show me iniquity, and cause me to see trouble? For plundering and violence are before me; there is strife, and contention arises. Therefore the law is powerless, and justice never goes forth. For the wicked surround the righteous; therefore perverse judgment proceeds."

As Habakkuk looked at his day, he was extremely frustrated by what he saw, just as you may find yourself to be when looking at what claims to be a "Christian nation." Our nation is filled with drugs, murder, violence, rape, and pornography, and sometimes we look at this country we treasure and we wonder how long God will sustain America without bringing judgment on it.

Habakkuk felt the same way about his nation, and his emotions were heavy on his heart, so he began to pray. In the beginning of his letter you can see that he felt God was being inattentive: "Lord, how long shall I cry out and you won't hear?" And the Lord was not only inattentive, but, from Habakkuk's perspective, He was indifferent to the problem. "How long will I cry out to You and You won't do anything? Here is a nation chosen by You, and they have turned their backs on You." Habakkuk names some of his nation's problems, including "slackened law and no judgment" literally, a delinquent court system. People got involved, were brought before the tribunal, and nothing happened.

Habakkuk, a righteous man, looks at the problem and cries out to God. Have you ever called out to the Lord and felt He didn't hear you? That He didn't care? You begin to wonder if there is something wrong with your prayers because nothing happens that you can see.

When God did respond to Habakkuk's prayer, the answer only served to confuse him. Perhaps you have had that experience. You call out to the Lord, He gives you direction, and you are more confused than ever!

The Lord tells Habakkuk in verse 5, "Look among the nations and watch—be utterly astounded! For I will work a work in your days which you would not believe, though it were told you." The Lord has decided to judge the wickedness of the Jews, but He says that He has chosen the nation of the Chaldeans to punish them. That was incredible, because the Chaldeans were the most wicked nation at that time. They killed babies, treated their women terribly, and were involved in every sort of evil. They were so bad that when God sent Jonah to preach to them in previous years, he didn't want to go. Yet now He says "I have heard you cry for judgment, so I have decided to get the Chaldeans to do the job for me."

Habakkuk just shakes his head. This makes no sense! Why would God use the most wicked nation on earth to judge His chosen people? The rest of the book is a dialogue between Habakkuk and God over that question.

HABAKKUK'S WONDERING

It is interesting to note that, as Habakkuk moved from his "whys" to his worship, he went through a time where he had difficult questions and no easy answers. "Are You not from everlasting, O Lord my God, my Holy One?" asks Habakkuk. "O Lord, you have appointed them for judgment; O Rock, You have marked them for correction. You are of purer eyes than to behold evil" (verses 12–13). Now stop and consider what Habakkuk did. He asks a question, yet he extols the virtues of God. He calls God eternal, holy, sovereign, mighty, and pure—even though he has no idea why God is working this way. He focuses on God even when he can't understand God's actions. He realizes that he does not understand, so he reviews the nature of God which he knows so well. He clings to what he knows to be true about God.

There is an important lesson there. When you are in the low point of life, facing times of discouragement and unanswered questions like Habakkuk, grab hold of the truths you know about God. Hang on to them with all your heart, like Habakkuk. Perhaps that is why his name means "the embracer"—in times of trial he embraces nothing but God. I have experienced some incredible highs and some terrible lows, and it was in those low periods that I prayed, "Lord, I don't know what is going on. But I do know You are a good God and You love me. Help me to hang on to those two facts today." If you are going through some low times now, grab hold of God's holiness, goodness, and love, and see if you can get through it by remembering who He is. Don't spend time meditating on your problems, that won't do any good. Get your eyes off your problems and onto the Lord. That's what Habakkuk did. He reviewed the nature of God. He stared in amazement and wonder at the beauty and majesty of God.

HABAKKUK'S WORSHIP

That is why, as you turn to the last chapter in the book, Habakkuk has gone from why to wonder to worship. Notice 3:17–19: "Though the fig tree may not blossom, nor fruit be on the vines; though the labor of the olive may fail, and the fields yield no food; though the flock may be cut off from the fold, and there be no herd in the stalls —yet I will rejoice in the Lord, I will joy in the God of my salvation. The Lord God is my strength; He will make my feet like deer's feet, and He will make me walk on my high hills." That is one of the most incredible passages in all of Scripture. It is like a man standing up in church after he has lost the most precious thing in all of his life and saying, as Job did, "Though He slay me, yet will I trust Him." I will worship God regardless of the circumstances and my understanding of them.

Habakkuk's worship transcends the circumstances. How could he be like that? Where does he find the inner strength to go from tragedy to triumph in three short chapters? Habakkuk understood one tremendous truth: You worship the One you trust, and you trust the One you know.

If we, as God's people, are going to be prepared for both the mountaintop and the valley experiences that are sure to touch our lives, we have got to learn how to worship God. We have got to learn to say, "I will rejoice in the Lord, the God of my salvation." But we will never be able to do that until we learn to trust Him with the unanswered questions. You see, you learn to trust Him when you come to know Him. When you know God, you learn in your heart that He is trustworthy. Because Habakkuk knew God, he trusted God. And because he trusted God, he worshiped Him.

The Bible was given to us so that we might know Jesus Christ, and have the passion of Paul, who said at the end of his life that his reason for living was that he might know Jesus. Does your Bible reading and study have as its goal to know Jesus? Does your quiet time of worship have as its focus to know Him better? If you don't know Him well, you can't trust Him, and you won't be able to worship Him fully.

The missionary Hudson Taylor made it a point to always be worshiping the Lord when the sun came up. Every morning, no matter how tired he was, Hudson Taylor spent time worshiping God. He said in his writings that the one thing that sustained him through all the difficulties he faced in China was the fact that in worshiping God he found strength for a new day. Hudson Taylor knew God, had learned to trust Him, and had a time of worship each day with Him to draw the energy to make it through another day.

As you consider all that God has done for you, do you not want to worship Him? Don't you desire to know Him better, to trust and rely on Him, and to find a calm assurance that, regardless of circumstances, He can guide you through this life? Worship God, and your life will never be the same.

1. Read Job 19:1–27.

    a. What is Job's chief complaint to his friends? (verses 1–3)

    b. What does he conclude about the possibility of his own sin being the cause of his suffering? (verse 4)

    c. Who does he also think may be to blame? (verse 6, 21)

    d. From verses 7–20, list all the complaints Job has about his present circumstances:

        • verse 7

        • verse 8

        • verse 9

        • verse 10

        • verses 11–12

        • verses 13–17

        • verses 18–19

        • verse 20

e. Why does he want his argument preserved permanently? (verses 23–24)

f. What does he ultimately believe will be his only vindication? (verses 25–27)

g. Though Job's perspective is colored by his frustration at this point, what application can you draw from his final conclusion about receiving justice?

h. What conclusion about his experience did Job finally come to? (Job 42:1–6)

i. What had Job been focused on that kept him from seeing God clearly in the beginning?

j. As far as we know, what information was Job ever given about the reasons and nature of his suffering? (see Job 1–2)

k. What does this tell us about whether we will always get our "Why" questions answered in this life?

l. Why is it "okay" if we don't get specific answers to our questions?

m. Cite an instance where you have had to rest in God alone because you have not received the answer to a "Why" question:

n. How difficult was it for you to release your "need to know" all the answers? What prompted you to rest wholly in Him?

o. If there has been a time you have struggled with "Why" as Job did, note that circumstance here—and what you learned through the experience:

2. Read Psalm 6:1–10.

a. What is David's cry to God? (verse 4)

b. What is he facing? (verse 5)

c. How does he express his confidence in God? (verses 8–9)

d. Is verse 10 written in past or future tense? How is verse 10 a statement of faith?

e. Is David living by sight or by faith as the psalm concludes? (2 Corinthians 5:7)

3. Read Psalm 13:1–6.

   a. What is David's repetitious question in this psalm? (verses 1–2)

   b. In what is David's confidence? (verse 5)

   c. For what does David worship God in spite of his present circumstances? (verse 6)

4. If there is a "Why, Lord?" issue in your life at the moment, write out a confession of confidence to God—a statement of trust in His purposes in spite of your circumstances:

DID YOU KNOW?

The most famous verse in Habakkuk is 2:4—"But the just shall live by his faith." The apostle Paul quotes this verse in Romans 1:17, "For in [the Gospel] the righteousness of God is revealed from faith to faith; as it is written, 'The just shall live by faith.'" This was the verse that opened the eyes of faith of a young Roman Catholic monk in Germany named Martin Luther. He had agonized for many months over the condition of his own sinful soul, wondering how he might find rest and assurance of salvation. His discovery that life was found, not in organized religion but in a faith relationship with God through Christ, sparked the Protestant Reformation in 1517.

ETERNAL PERSPECTIVE

Selected Scriptures

*In this lesson we discover how to develop
an eternal perspective on life.*

OUTLINE

For some people, life consists of managing the mountainous events which come up every day. For others, however, those events are just the "small stuff" of life. Not that they aren't important—but they pale in significance when viewed in light of eternity.

I. **The Illustration**
   A. The Opportunities in John's Life
   B. The Obstacles in John's Life
   C. The Open Door in John's Life

II. **The Invitation**
   A. An Invitation to New Power
   B. An Invitation to New Perspective

III. **The Instruction**
   A. Praise God Through Music
   B. Praise God Through Scripture Memory
   C. Praise God in Daily Intervals
   D. Praise God Through Visual Reminders
   E. Praise God Through a Small Group

IV. **The Inspiration**

> IN PREPARATION FOR THIS LESSON, BE SURE TO READ CHAPTER FIFTEEN
> IN THE BOOK, *My Heart's Desire.*

Paul Azinger was a championship golfer on the PGA tour when, at age 33, he was diagnosed with cancer. He had won ten PGA tournaments and was at the top of his game. He was shaken by the diagnosis of a life-threatening disease and wrote these words: "A genuine feeling of fear came over me. I could die from cancer. Then another reality hit me even harder. I'm going to die eventually anyway, whether from cancer or something else. It's just a question of when. Everything I had accomplished in golf became meaningless to me. All I wanted to do was live."

A friend of Azinger's, Larry Moody, who taught Bible studies for golfers on the PGA tour, said something to him that changed his whole perspective: "Zinger, we're not in the land of the living and heading for the land of the dying. We're in the land of the dying trying to get to the land of the living." That statement caused him to reevaluate his whole life. He gained new courage to fight the cancer, and eventually made his way back to professional golf. What he wrote following his bout with cancer revealed a much deeper perspective on life: "I've made a lot of money since I've been on the tour, and I've won a lot of tournaments, but that happiness is always temporary. The only way you will ever have true contentment is in a personal relationship with Jesus Christ. I'm not saying that nothing ever bothers me and I don't have problems, but I feel like I've found the answer to the six foot hole."

Most people, in fact many Christians, live as if this life is the land of the living—that this is our permanent home, as good as it gets. They strive and work to get all the gusto they can out of this life since the next life is cloaked in mystery. But we should have an accurate perspective on this life and the next. We have God's Word to teach us, and we spend time worshiping Him in His very presence. We should have no fears at all about the culmination of this life and the glorious life that awaits us. Having had my own brush with cancer, I know how such an experience can deepen one's perception of the true meaning of life.

If we do not develop an eternal perspective and learn to view this life in light of eternity, we will miss the key to worshiping God every moment of our lives.

THE ILLUSTRATION

There is no better example of a man with an eternal perspective than John the Apostle—especially in the years following Christ's ascension to heaven.

The Opportunities in John's Life

John, along with Peter and James, was part of an inner circle among the twelve disciples. John was with Jesus at critical moments in His life such as the Garden of Gethsemane (Matthew 26:36–37) and the crucifixion (John 19:25–27). It was John who outran Peter on the way to the empty tomb on Resurrection morning (John 20:3–4). He was also present with Peter and James on the Mount of Transfiguration when Jesus was glorified in their presence (Matthew 17:1–2). He was there when Jesus ascended into heaven (Acts 1:9) and then received a powerful revelation from Christ when the door of heaven was opened before him (Revelation 4:1a). He was witness to the mighty power and majesty of the throne of God. As much as anyone, John's eyes had been opened to the eternal origin and destination of the Son of God—and how those who believed in Him would follow Him to heaven one day.

The Obstacles in John's Life

In spite of John's opportunities, he also faced many obstacles. He endured a Roman exile on the island of Patmos at a critical time in the life of the early Church (Revelation 1:9). He probably lived much of that time not knowing the fate of his fellow apostles, whether they were alive or had been martyred for Jesus' sake. He did not know his own fate either. After all, Jesus had told the disciples that they must drink from the same cup from which He was destined to drink (Matthew 20:23). Death was clearly what Jesus referred to—but John knew not the time or the manner in which He would suffer for Jesus.

While John watched the years of his latter life tick by, he was like all of us in a sense. All of us are exiles, aliens and strangers in this world, citizens of another "country" (Philippians 3:20; 1 Peter 2:11). But John's exile was pronounced—absent from friends, apart from the church, longing to be released from exile and rejoined with Jesus his Lord. But one day his lonely exile was interrupted by the opening of a door—into heaven!

The Open Door in John's Life

The light of heaven shown through a door which had not been there before—"a door was opened in heaven" (Revelation 4:1, KJV). One moment, the elderly John might well have been lamenting his rheumatism, or he might have been tossing and turning through another restless night. His thoughts might have been on absent friends as they faced trial or prison. Perhaps he was reliving the wonderful days of Jesus' physical presence and wishing that time hadn't passed so quickly. If he was anything like you and me, John was immersed in the disappointments of this world, the land of the dead. And then, when the door was suddenly thrown open, John walked through the portal to an eternal perspective.

THE INVITATION

John was given a view into heaven in order to write it down so that we might have the same view. The same Jesus who beckoned John to "come up hither" beckons us to come also. He wants us to stand before the throne of God and worship in the freedom which only an eternal perspective can give.

An Invitation to New Power

John was a changed man after getting a heavenly perspective, as were Paul Azinger and countless others. Seeing the difference between the land of the dead and the land of the living makes all the difference. Learning to worship—to live as if we are already in the land of the living—can bring life into the land of the dead.

Worship and praise of God is the great work of humanity in this life, but that doesn't mean an abandonment of normal life and work. Instead, worship transforms our work into something new. Dwelling in the presence of the King bathes us in a new perspective for life on this earth. As the hymn says, "The things of earth will grow strangely dim in the light of His glory and grace."

An Invitation to New Perspective

The great Christian apologist, C. S. Lewis, wrote an allegory called *The Great Divorce*. In it, a man rides a bus to paradise and finds it is more fully and powerfully real than anything he could have imagined. Everything is alive, bursting with color, and expressed in complete reality. But hell, he discovers, is nothing more than a fleck of dust in comparison. It is concerned only with tiny things. In the same way, Lewis suggests, our lives in this world become smaller and smaller in light of the grandness of eternity.

Revelation 4 gives us the same impression. Everything John sees is grand in scale, gigantic in proportion. First we wonder at it all, then we worship. Suddenly everything in this world becomes small and insignificant in comparison. Getting a glimpse of heaven is like standing on the edge of the Grand Canyon, or at the top of the Rocky Mountains, and being speechless at the sight. We suddenly see that God is much bigger than we had thought—and wants bigger and better things for us than this world can offer. Worship is where we get that glimpse of heaven that can change our lives.

How can we get a glimpse of heaven like John had and bring our lives on this earth into proper perspective?

THE INSTRUCTION

In Colossians 3:1–2 Paul tells us to set our minds on eternal things, not earthly ones: "Set your affection on things above, not on things on the earth" (KJV). We have been raised with Christ and seated positionally with Him in the heavenlies (Colossians 3:1, 3). Why then should we get comfortable in the gutters of this world?

While all of this sounds spiritual and high-minded, we still have bills to pay, jobs to do, families to care for. How do we maintain this spiritual perspective in light of our constant interaction with the systems and demands of this worldly life we lead? It is by incorporating worship into our everyday lifestyle. Taking part in worship once a week at church on Sunday is not enough, which may be why many Christians struggle to keep a heavenly perspective. The Spirit of God is with us wherever we go, so we can remain in an attitude of worship wherever we are.

Here are some practical ways to jumpstart your life of praise and worship. This is not an exhaustive list, but it is a practical one. These ideas will sharpen your heavenly perspective immediately if you will implement them.

Praise God Through Music

Oh come, let us sing to the Lord! Let us shout joyfully to the Rock of our salvation.

Let us come before His presence with thanksgiving; Let us shout joyfully to Him with psalms.

For the Lord is the great God, And the great King above all gods. (Psalm 95:1–3)

Music of worship and praise is a core part of maintaining my own heavenly perspective. Choose a CD of praise music that really ministers to you and immerse yourself in it for a week. Staying with the same songs for an extended period allows you to focus over and over on the words; the music has time to soothe your soul and lift your spirit. After a week you'll know the words by heart and you'll be able to sing the songs yourself wherever you are when you're away from the music itself.

Praise God Through Scripture Memory

Your word I have hidden in my heart,

That I might not sin against You! (Psalm 119:11)

Don't groan inwardly at this suggestion. I know it is basic, but there is no task more worthy of your time than learning fundamental truths "by heart." Once those verses are embedded in your heart they become part of you. They are there at all times for the Holy Spirit to use to encourage you and guide you. Memorizing any Scripture verse is profitable (2 Timothy 3:16) but for the purpose we're discussing here, I suggest you memorize passages like Revelation 4 or Psalm 100—great passages which focus on worship and praise of God.

All of us have heard stories of prisoners of war who were able to remain faithful and hopeful by recalling Scriptures they had memorized as a child. Your Bible can be taken from you but your memory is yours forever.

Praise God in Daily Intervals

Seven times a day I praise You,

Because of Your righteous judgments. (Psalm 119:164)

Most of us are familiar with the idea of a daily quiet time or morning devotions. While those are essential as a matter of discipline and consistency in spiritual growth, our goal as Christians is to praise and worship God all day long. A helpful pattern is to build into your life times when you can praise God often during the day. If you have morning and afternoon "coffee breaks" at work, a lunch hour, times when you are driving to and from work, all of those represent regular moments when you can turn your attention to God and worship Him in the midst of your day. Carrying Bible verses on cards, or a pocket New Testament, is a way to keep the Word at hand at all times.

Praise God Through Visual Reminders

For Your loving kindness is before my eyes . . . (Psalm 26:3a).

Reminders are things like refrigerator magnets, coffee mugs, or pictures we keep nearby. We keep them handy for a variety of reasons in life, and there's no reason not to use them as motivators to worship God. The dashboard of your car, the bathroom mirror, and your desk at work are good places to post memory verses, devotional sayings, or motivational pictures or images. Every time you see one of these, you'll be reminded to stop and offer exaltation and thanksgiving to your God.

Praise God Through a Small Group

"So continuing daily with one accord in the temple, and breaking bread from house to house, they ate their food with gladness and simplicity of heart, praising God and having favor with all the people. And the Lord added to the church daily those who were being saved" (Acts 2:46–47).

Talk to some likeminded friends who share your desire to be more devoted to worship and gather with them once a week at a convenient time to focus on praise and worship together. Most of the time we emphasize Bible study in these groups, and that's fine. We need to be doing that, too, of course. But perhaps your group can take a period of time to reorient yourselves a bit more in the direction of worship. If you work in an office, you might find a partner or small group of believers who will meet you fifteen minutes before work each day so you can praise God together.

I guarantee that if you'll try at least one or two of these initiatives, your life will be changed. Your anxiety will melt away. You'll be worshiping gladly, and you'll begin to be conformed to the image of Christ.

THE INSPIRATION

I heard about an elderly man who worked in the evenings cleaning office buildings. Jim, an executive in a building cleaned by the old gentleman, would see the janitor on nights he worked late. Jim was constantly under stress, working long hours, and was intrigued by the infectious smile on the old man's face. One night Jim asked the janitor what allowed him to smile when all he had to look forward to was cleaning bathrooms and floors.

"It's a little lonely," the janitor replied. "But Jesus is with me whenever I need Him. Maybe I'd feel different about cleaning bathrooms if Jesus wasn't with me. But think about it—Jesus is here the whole time, and we converse while I work. Plus, I get paid!"

Practicing the presence of Christ will give you an eternal perspective. The situations of this life will get smaller and smaller as heaven gets bigger in your eyes.

1. Read Philippians 3:20–21.

    a. If you are traveling in a foreign country, what does it mean when you tell someone your citizenship is American? What are the implications of citizenship?

    b. How do you live differently in a country in which you are a traveler versus one in which you have citizenship? Name as many differences as you can (for example, where you live, etc.).

    c. What are the implications of permanence versus "temporary-ness"?

    d. If you are a Christian, where is your citizenship? (verse 20)

    e. What word best describes your perception of your time on earth if your citizenship is in heaven?

    f. When will we begin to enjoy residency in our permanent home "country"? (verse 21)

    g. Why is a transformation of our body necessary before going to live in our home country? (verse 21)

h. What does that suggest to you about the differences in the two worlds?

2. What practical things do you do to prove to yourself that this world is really not your home?

   a. What signs do you see occasionally that you are getting more tied to this world than to the world to come?

   b. What do you think is the biggest reason the Church at large doesn't live with more of an eternal perspective?

   c. How would the church in America be different if her perspective were heavenly instead of earthly?

3. How would you relate the parable in Matthew 13:44 to the challenge of living with a heavenly perspective?

   a. What trait characterized the man when he discovered the treasure in the field?

   b. How much joy does the average Christian have over discovering the kingdom of God and eternal life?

c. In practical terms, what does it mean to "sell all you have" in order not to lose your focus on the kingdom of heaven?

d. In light of this parable, what does Matthew 6:21 contribute to the discussion of maintaining an eternal perspective?

e. Would you rather have treasure on earth or treasure in heaven?

f. How literally should we take Jesus' words in Matthew 19:21; Mark 10:21; and Luke 18:22?

g. How important is remaining divested of this world's goods to keeping an eternal perspective?

4. Note how the concept of "aliens and strangers" is used in progressively different ways from the Old Testament to the New Testament:

a. Leviticus 25:23

b. Psalm 39:12

c. Ephesians 2:19

d. Hebrews 11:13

e. 1 Peter 1:17

f. 1 Peter 2:11

5. What part of returning "home" do you most look forward to?
   And what aspect of this world do you least regret having to
   leave behind?

DID YOU KNOW?

P salms 120–134 are called the "songs of ascents." It is thought
that these songs would be sung by Jewish worshipers as
they made their way from their tribal areas up to the city of
Jerusalem three times a year for the great feasts (see Psalm 42:4;
122:4; Isaiah 30:29). The only way these worshipers could travel
over rough roads, manage children and animals, and sing at the
same time was to know these psalms "by heart." The repetition of
worshipful music stores it in the mind, making it available for recall
at times of worship.

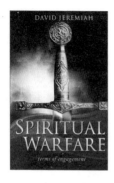

Spiritual Warfare

The strategies of our enemy are not strong enough to withstand the spiritual armor that God has given us. In this series, Dr. David Jeremiah shows us how to use the six-piece suit of armor against spiritual warfare. Although the enemy is out to attack, Christ has already won the battle that we face. This study helps us better understand that we need to stay clothed in spiritual armor in order to lead a victorious life.

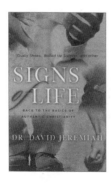

Signs of Life

Our health can be determined by our vital "signs of life." In *Signs of Life,* Dr. David Jeremiah gives five signs of spiritual life—the condition of our shoes, knees, sleeves, hands, and arms—that we should use to determine how we live our lives and influence those around us. In this practical study, Dr. Jeremiah explains these vital signs and shows us how live a more vibrant spiritual life.

Prayer the Great Adventure

"The Lord's Prayer" is a model that we can use to pray effectively. Jesus gave His followers this prayer in order to show them the importance of praise and how to stay connected with the Lord. In *Prayer the Great Adventure*, we learn how to practice effective prayer, implement the Lord's teaching in our lives, grow closer to God, and thank Him for all He has done.

Each of these resources was created from a teaching series by Dr. David Jeremiah. Additional resources are available at www.DavidJeremiah.org

For pricing information and ordering, contact us at

P.O. Box 3838
San Diego, CA 92163
(800) 947-1993
WWW.DAVIDJEREMIAH.ORG

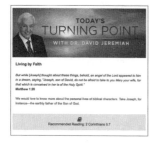